Harry always was a Crap Hat

By Brian (Harry) Clacy

This book is dedicated to Mr Barnes, who, from 1971 until 1974 was my English teacher at Broomfield Secondary Modern School just outside Chelmsford in Essex. Mr Barnes was a short, tubby, balding and wonderful teacher who had a thin military style moustache; he alone somehow managed to get a total fuckwit like me to enjoy reading books.

CONTENTS

As a boy
Death of a French Dignitary
Warts and all
Susan will go to university
Forever blowing bubbles
How much to buy your sister
A bit of a slip up
Bullseye
Better than Subuteo
It's an army life for me

As a soldier
Oath of Allegiance
A Royal visit
Captain McCloud SAS
Hannah Gordon's bottom
Convoy Cock
Just a bit of shit
Exercise Spearpoint
Don't mess with the RCT
Casualty list
Ballykinler beach
Black Saracen Awards
What would your mother think
I think he's dead
Lieutenant Colonel Bell RAMC
Ex Dentibus Ensis

<u>As a Civil Servant</u>
Ruth and the Dickheads
Retinal Screening
The Commandants' curtains
Nuisance phone calls
Hypos
Tracy gets caught out
Where's Dave Gone
Royal Marines Division
One last nuisance phone call
Epilogue

Acknowledgements

This book has been quite difficult to write, as are most sequels I suppose, after receiving many emails and messages on Facebook when my books 'Harry was a Crap Hat' and 'Two Medics One Nurse and a Gob Doctor' were published, I was worried 'Harry always was a Crap Hat' might be a huge disappointment. I really do hope you the reader don't find it so, everything you are about to read in this book is absolutely true in almost every detail and goes to show there is humour in the everyday things we do and say. We Brits are interesting people and as a nation we are renowned for our sometimes macabre and ironic sense of humour, I have met many humorous people in my everyday life and a lot of them are included in this very book, some names have been changed to protect the very guilty.

I would like to thank the following people who have helped and encouraged me in writing this book and I apologise to my good friends Adam Broom and Dave Burr for taking so long to get the job done.

June Bell and Grace Irwin are members of my Yorkshire 'octogenarian' and 'septuagenarian' fan clubs respectively, I say fan clubs, these two are the only members. Along with my mother-in-law Joyce Chapman, they both kindly agreed to proof read it, I can't believe this trio didn't mind reading the chapter called 'Convoy Cock'.

My neighbour and friend Carol Baines who came up with the title 'Bullseye' for one of the chapters, I was going to call the chapter 'One Hundred and Eighty' but 'Bullseye' was an inspired idea. See what you think when you read it.

Vanessa Spong for her information about the QARANC's and for pointing out that women often don't get a proper mention in the macho bullshit world of the Armed Forces. Sorry mate.

I would also like to mention Cefn Bartlett and Andrew Gardner who both served in 10 Regiment RCT with me, their Facebook notes were an invaluable contribution to the book, as were all the emails from my old RADC comrade Steve Roberts.

Many thanks must go to my sisters Trisha and Susan and also to my incredibly witty brother David, I should apologise for the way I treated you all when we were younger, but fuck me they were funny days. I would like to give a massive thanks to Eric Hartley and Laura Murrell of ELK Marketing who have done a fabulous job in creating this book cover.

My friend Colin Handley has been my tormentor for many years as we worked together in the Civil Service; he has an incredible memory and sometimes cruel sense of humour, without him there wouldn't be a Civil Service part to this book.

Last but by no means least I must thank the person who kicked this whole literary thing off in the first place, my beautiful wife Nicky.

Introduction

If you haven't read my first book 'Harry was a Crap Hat', please don't panic, you can still read this one and then go out and buy the first one later. Just make sure you do buy it though because it really is a fantastic read. The problem with reading this one initially is that you won't know what the fuck a 'Crap Hat' is, so I will now give you a short résumé. Here goes.

I joined the Junior Leaders Regiment of the Royal Corps of Transport in May of 1974 at the tender age of sixteen years old; the army training was an eighteen-month initiation to a life in the Regular British Army. At Norton Manor Camp just outside Taunton in Somerset, my fellow recruits and I would be trained and educated to become soldiers, and possible future Senior Non Commissioned Officers of our Corps. You know the sort of characters I'm talking about, we were being shaped to become the Corps loud-mouthed Sergeants and Sergeant Majors of the future, men who didn't know their arse from their elbow but were capable of beating the shit out of Jean-Claude Van Damme.

After lights out on my first night in the dormitory room in Dalton Troop, a gobby Yorkshire lad nicknamed me Harry Toplip referring to my slight overbite. I wouldn't mind but he had teeth the size of tombstones and a hairstyle not dissimilar to Bet Lynch in the Rovers Return. Still, he got a lot of laughs as the name spread throughout the camp over the coming days and everyone started doing their rabbit teeth impressions whenever they saw me: my mum used to tell me, "If anyone takes the Mickey out of you, it is only because they are jealous." My mum wasn't one of the greatest philosophers the world has ever seen and the advice didn't help get the cruel bastards off my back, I also didn't get much comfort from my mum's other words of wisdom. "While they are picking on you son, they are leaving someone else alone." Most of the time; I wanted to be someone else. Anyway, that is how I was re-christened with the name Harry when my real name is Brian.

Now for the Crap Hat bit. On completion of our training in Taunton, all the recruits who stayed the course and survived the bullying by our fellow recruits then got to choose which trade they wanted to serve in within the Royal Corps of Transport. The choices were quite varied; you could become either a General Transport Driver, Bandsman, Air Dispatcher, Train Driver, Hovercraft Operator, Clerk, Paratrooper, Driver/Radio Operator or last but by no means least, you could work as a Port Operator down at 17 Port and Maritime Regiment RCT in Southampton.

My Corporal instructor in the final stages of my training was a bloke called Pete Young, he had come to our training unit from 63 Parachute Squadron RCT, 63 Para were the transport support element of 5 Airborne Brigade. RCT soldiers who wanted to wear the coveted maroon beret of the airborne forces and serve in 63 Para had to go through the agony of the P Company selection course; all airborne troops have to pass P Company to become a Paratrooper. Pete Young was my hero and I wanted to become an RCT Paratrooper just like him, so I went on the dreaded 'beat up' course at 63 Parachute Squadron RCT in Aldershot. We were accommodated in the transit block in Buller Barracks and from day one we were beasted by a Corporal from 63 Squadron RCT to see if we were fit and tough enough to go on the feared P Company Course. By day four I had had enough, British Paratroopers are the toughest and damn near the fittest soldiers in the world and there was no way I could achieve the standard required to win that maroon beret. The majority of British Troops are tough and robust but paratroopers are in a whole different league, and they know it, which is why they are so proud of the beret they wear. The rest of the British Army wears a very dark blue beret, which the Airborne Forces think isn't a very good form of headdress; in fact they think it is a 'Crap Hat'. Anyone serving outside of the Airborne Forces is therefore called a 'Crap Hat', or if the particular paratrooper you are facing is pissed and angry, he will just call you a 'Hat' before knocking your teeth out. Hence why I called my first book 'Harry was a 'Crap Hat'. I spent the next eighteen odd years in the army serving firstly as a General Transport Driver in the RCT before getting injured in Northern Ireland, after which I became an RCT Regimental Medical Assistant and then transferring to the Royal Army Dental Corps.

This book will go into more details of my life as a child, as a soldier and eventually as a Civil Servant within the Ministry of Defence, with every turn of the page you will begin to understand why, 'Harry always was a Crap Hat'.

AS A BOY

As a boy I grew up in a large family that lived in a lot of garrison towns around the world, my father joined the Devon and Dorset infantry Regiment in 1944 but failed to see any action in World War Two. His chance of getting into some blood guts and glory did eventually come though when he served out in the Far East during the Malayan Emergency in the 1950's. He and the rest of the Commonwealth Forces were tasked with hunting down the MNLA (Malayan National Liberation Army) who were the military arm of the Malayan Communist Party. My father sweated his arse off carrying a Bren gun and spare magazines full of live ammunition, he tramped through snake infested swamps and thick jungle vegetation fighting against the CT's (Communist Terrorists). It was whilst hearing mortar rounds fly over his head that he deduced, "The life of an infantryman is shit." He was an Acting Lance Corporal when he asked for an interview with his Company Commander; my father had read on Company Orders that the Military Provost Staff Corps (Military Prison Wardens) were trying to recruit soldiers from other regiments because the MPSC was undermanned. If he was successful in getting a transfer and passed the MPSC trade training course, he would automatically be promoted to Sergeant and would never again have to live the life of a nomadic tramp. He put in his transfer request and was interviewed by his Company Commander who had served with the infantry throughout the Second World War, the Major obviously knew how awful life was in the infantry and at the same time concluded just how shit an infantryman my father was, he therefore endorsed my dad's transfer request to an easier life in the British Army.

My mother on the other hand was an RAF Dental Nurse, and whilst serving out in Egypt she got herself an Australian boyfriend who was serving on the Air Sea Rescue Helicopters. Mum's boyfriend had been infuriated by an officer within his unit after they both got involved in a unit fracas; a few days later the boyfriend stole a .303 Lee Enfield Rifle and some ammunition from his unit armoury and used the afore mentioned officer for a bit of target practice. We all know what these antipodean's are like when they've had a few too many. Anyway, the Commonwealth Courts Martial Centre took a pretty dim view of his poor marksmanship skills and they decreed that he should be sent to the military prison in Egypt, he was put in the safe custody of my dad (who had recently transferred into the MPSC) to await his transportation home to Australia. Convict Deportation was a subject on which his ancestors may have been able to give him a good insight. Whilst my mum visited her psychotic, but by now sober Aussie boyfriend, she met Sergeant Clacy in the MPSC guardroom. Sergeant Clacy knew that the Aussie was going to be out of the way for the next couple of years and immediately smoothed his way into my mum's life. When my dad realised my mum was a nice girl and that she wouldn't sleep with him, not without a valid wedding licence or some chloroform, he got down on one knee and proposed.

They were married out in Egypt and over the following years they had four children, Trisha, the first born of the Clacy plebs (person lacking even basic skills) arrived in Yeovil Hospital in Somerset, Susan was then born in the British Military Hospital in Hong Kong, and next I arrived when my dad was posted back to Shepton Mallet Military Prison in Somerset. My brother was born in the British Military Hospital out in Dhekelia Garrison Cyprus in 1964 six years after I was hatched; we other three kids repeatedly made him cry when we told him he was a romantic after thought. Don't feel sorry for him, at the age of four he didn't even know what a romantic after thought was and yet he still bawled his eyes out.

The next part of this book will give you all the missing anecdotes that weren't included in 'Harry was a Crap Hat', about my life in the Clacy family as a boy.

DEATH OF A FRENCH DIGNITARY

Napoleon was dead. No, not the rotund and vertically challenged French Emperor in the funny hat, I'm talking about my pet black and white mouse Napoleon. I held his cold and stiff corpse in my hands and wailed as only an eight year old can. "Why? Oh why had the Lord taken him from me?" My mother bluntly put me in the picture, "Because you never fed him and he probably starved to death. Better pop him in the bin love, I think he's starting to smell a bit ripe." Not one for getting over emotional was my old mum! She was right about me not feeding him regularly though; in fact he got so thin at times that he could escape through the bars of his cage and he started to eat the Encyclopaedia Britannica books Granny Bryant had given us. I had to go through the painful ordeal of organising his funeral.

My father had left the British Army 18 month previously after serving most of his military career in the MPSC (Military Provost Staff Corps), growing up on army camps as a child had turned me into an 'Army Barmy' young schoolboy. I had a small section of Action Men armed with a variety of weapons and equipment that I sent out on endless suicide missions, somehow they always returned battered and bruised but victorious. At night I posted one of my lads on sentry duty outside my bedroom door with his rifle held in the sloped arms position, he was there to protect me and deter my evil older sisters from sneaking up and attacking me. In the morning I usually found the 'Evil Ones' had pulled his trousers down and bent him over so he was mooning at me as I came out of my bedroom. You can call me harsh if you like but even though I knew his abuminable, sorry, I mean abominable actions were done under duress; I still placed him on a charge and gave him extra duties.

With all this military background and idealism installed in my head I felt compelled to give Napoleon a burial with full military honours. I found a large empty matchbox and lined it with the Izal greaseproof toilet paper my father had pinched from his workplace at Her Majesty's Prison Chelmsford. Napoleon looked peaceful but gaunt as I slide the box shut. In the garage I found two pieces of wood and a six-inch nail that made a suitable cross to mark his final resting place.

I know Napoleon would have wanted it, so I asked my sisters if they would take part in the funeral procession, all three of us would slow-march down to the end of the garden where the already prepared grave was located. Susan would lead the funeral party singing 'Jerusalem', I would be next carrying the dearly departed like a waiter carrying a tray of drinks and Trish would bring up the rear carrying the wreath. I had a bit of luck with the wreath as it happens, someone's father had been buried in Fordham cemetery that very morning and so I borrowed one from his grave; I felt he had more than enough and poor old Napoleon had none. Trisha looked demure as she slow marched down the garden path carrying the yellow chrysanthemum wreath that spelt out the word 'DAD'. After lowering his body into the ground we bowed our heads in a minutes silence, this was broken when Trisha said, "How much longer are we doing this crap for? The High Chaparral is on TV in a minute". We retired to the Sergeants Mess in the kitchen for digestive biscuits and banana flavoured Nesquick.

The local vicar was not as amused as our father about the 'borrowed' wreath and he gave me a 200 yard exclusion zone from the church and its surrounding area, unfortunately this ban was lifted for one hour every Sunday so I could attend Sunday School classes. He was probably praying for me in the hope that I would see the light and change my mischievous ways with a bit of Religious Education. He must still be praying now though because it hasn't worked.

Napoleon's funeral had been planned and executed with a minimum of fuss and expense and my mum said I had done him proud. We discussed the death in some detail but she cut short our conversation when she said, "No you can't have a bloody puppy!"

WARTS AND ALL

As a child I had large ugly warts that grew on both of my hands, and children being children, my fellow pupils at school were particularly cruel and often shunned me with shouts of "LEPER!" My best friend Derek Davis usually rose above this and he didn't mind sitting next to me on the school bus. Derek and I were forever playing football with a heavy laced up leather football, if you headed it when it was soaking wet it was comparable to getting head butted by Vinnie Jones. I blame that football for my very poor academic achievements. If we couldn't be bothered to walk all the way up to Fordham village green, we would use a tennis ball and the small drains built into the kerbstones in the road outside our house were used as goals. As a West Ham United fan I was always either Bobby Ferguson in goal or Geoff Hurst when trying to put the ball in the back of the drain. Derek was a Newcastle United supporter until Arsenal got in the Final of the FA Cup and he changed his allegiance, he was then Bob Wilson in goal and Charlie George as a Striker. One of our legendary FA Cup Final matches at Wembley ended Arsenal 37 – West Hall United 34 before we were called in for tea. West Ham losing was a theme I would eventually have to get used to.

My mother and I had tried all sorts of cures from all sorts of people to try and get rid of my warts; we visited the doctor and he tried a freezing treatment that never worked and we also tried the utterly ridiculous mythological attempt of rubbing them with a pretty stone and then throwing it away. My aunt was a lovely woman but frigging useless at solving dermatological problems. I fell out with my mate Derek one day and we had a fight in the middle of Hall Road outside my house, I had him pinned down with my knees on his shoulders but was uncertain what I was supposed to do to bring the fight to a conclusion as he struggled underneath me. I looked up and saw my Dad in our sitting room window raising and lowering his fist into his other hand; he was demonstrating the art of punching someone's lights out. It was the only time in my life that I can remember my Dad taking any interest in anything I was doing, I felt a bond with the 'Old Man' for the first time in my life. I felt such a warm glow in the pit of my stomach, my dad was finally taking an interest in something I was doing and this alone inspired me to fill in my best mate's face.

As I pounded my clenched fists into poor old Derek's face I suddenly had a red mist descend over me, I had caught one of my warts on the right fore finger on his teeth and the wart had been ripped off down to the root. I started crying because of the pain, humiliation and pent up anger inside me and suddenly became aware of my dad dragging me off Derek and shouting, "That's enough! For Christ's sake that is enough!" Both Derek and I were now sobbing and howling like a couple of pregnant women watching a Bette Midler film.

My dad made us both shakes hands and took us into our kitchen to clean ourselves up and he put a plaster on my bleeding finger, he then sent Derek home. The old man congratulated me, "Bloody hell son, I though you were going to kill him, well done" By the end of the week Derek and I were best friends again and the fight had been forgotten about except for the wart that had been ripped off during the scuffle. The following day I was taken to see the doctor and my mum asked if it was possible to surgically remove all the remaining warts in one go, the only other option she could think of was for my dad to encourage my friend to just bite the damn things off. I was admitted to the main hospital in Colchester as an outpatient and had the remaining warts removed under a General Anaesthetic and bizarrely, thanks to my best friend Derek Davis biting and eating one of my warts, I have never been plagued with them again.

SUSAN WILL GO TO UNIVERSITY

Mrs Goody was the headmistress at Fordham Junior School where my sister and I attended, My God! If ever there was a woman wrongly named it was she. This harridan was the nastiest piece of work you could ever have the misfortune to meet as a schoolboy. She can best be described as a cross between Cruella Deville and the Wicked Witch of the West; she was an old skinny woman with grey hair that was tied up in a bun on the top of her head. It seemed to me that her primary job in the educational system was to sneer over the top of her spectacles and terrify me as much as she could. This woman was the epitome of a vindictive and iniquitous Victorian school headmistress. I used to tremble when I was called out to the front of the class and had to stand next to her desk, we all took turns in having to recite, from memory, any one of the twelve times tables. The look of distain on her face when I got any wrong was only surpassed if I actually got them all right. As I took the long walk up to her desk at the front of the class I would mutter under my breath, "Not the nine times table, please God, don't make it the nine times table." Everyone knows the nine times table is the hardest of all the multiplication tables. Mrs Goody would smirk at me and say, "Well Brian, let's see if you have managed to remember any of the... NINE TIMES TABLES." I would then think 'Oh flippin heck', which in the 1960's was the popular modern day schoolboy version of 'Oh fuck'.

At a parent/teacher night Mrs Goody extolled the good news about the academic brilliance of my year older sister Susan, "She is very bright and enthusiastic in the entire curriculum and remains top in most of the subjects. Mr and Mrs Clacy,

I feel sure that young Susan will have the intelligence and aptitude to go to university in the latter stages of her education." My dad apparently looked very pleased and smug at this fantastic report, a child that had spawned from his very own loins had obviously inherited his academic acumen. The reality was that if Susan had inherited any intelligence it must surely have come from our mum. Dad was as thick as two short planks. He then asked, "What about our Brian, how is he getting along?" Mrs Goody took a deep breath and sighed, "Well, the good news for you is that we will always need people to sweep the roads for us."

Told you she was a nasty piece of work.

FOREVEVER BLOWING BUBBLES

Like all British boys I started playing football at a young age but I didn't know anything about any particular football team; with my dad as a role model I was most likely to end up a piano accordion playing womaniser. The only sport my dad ever took part in was Judo and he won his green belt whilst serving in the British Army. He did do something that got him hot and sweaty though, he became a Ball Room Dance instructor when he was posted out to the Military Prison in Dhekelia Cyprus. I am sure he only took this up as a way of getting his grubby mitts on other women without raising suspicions with my mum. With regard to his musical talents, even today in my subconscious, many years later, I can still hear those strangled opening bars of 'She's a lassie from Lancashire' that escaped from the garage in Fordham where he practiced.

My dad hated sport so much that whilst on his Prison Officers Training Course after leaving the army, he made excuse after excuse to get out of any sort of physical training. My dad's truancy from training runs had not gone unnoticed by the training staff and they told him that he would fail the course if he did not attend the last cross country race on the penultimate day of the course. He thought that as he had got out of most of the training, the last six mile muddy run was a small price to pay to get a pass. All the trainee Prison Officers were to run in pairs starting at five minute intervals around a clearly marked route that went through muddy fields and across waist high rivers, their run would be monitored at six staging posts around the route by the permanent staff. On the day of the race my dad turned up at the start point at his designated time of 1030 hours and he was shouted at by the attending training instructor, "Where the bloody hell have you been Mr Clacy, all start times were brought forward by five minutes and your race partner has started without you!" My dad apologised and explained that no one had told him of the revised timings and also he had been sent on a mundane job that took him about half an hour to complete. As my dad and his already departed partner were the last competitors to leave he allowed my dad to start on his own and noted that he had started with a five-minute delay. The instructor shouted after my dad "Keep pushing yourself, with a good pace you should catch your partner up." When he got to the one-mile checkpoint my dad was out of puff and red faced as he had tried very hard to catch up with his partner. The instructor at the checkpoint was packing things away, he said "Ah! Mr Clacy, I though you weren't taking part in today's activity, your partner is only about four minutes ahead of you, keep pushing hard and I think you'll catch him. Well done!" My dad pushed himself harder and harder through each checkpoint until he got to the last checkpoint but one and was told he was only about a minute and a half behind his partner. He was covered in mud and his hands were freezing cold because of the driving winter rain and he was also on the point of collapse through sheer exhaustion. The last two hundred meters of the run was along the eight-foot high Training Centre perimeter wall, at the end of the wall he turned right into the main entrance in a state of near collapse. All the course students and instructors were lined up in Dress Uniforms and they clapped and cheered my dad over the finishing line, he had been set up, there had been no race and everyone in the training centre had been in on the joke. My dad was furious and stormed off shouting "You bastards!" My Dad had a great sense of humour about anything but himself. At the end of course presentations my dad was called forward to receive a prize for the most effort put into the final cross country race, he stepped up and shook the Commandants hand and was presented with a shoebox that contained a new pair of 'State of the art' training shoes. When he took them out of the box he noticed that someone had cut out the soles of the shoes. He had the good grace to laugh.

So bearing all this in mind, you have to wonder where my love of football comes from; the short answer is from my friends. A lot of young lads follow in their father's footsteps in regards to the football team they support, in my case I followed in the footsteps of my friend Gary Miller and his dad; he and Gary were ardent West Ham United supporters. When I asked them where West Ham United Football Club was they both laughed and told me it was in the East End of London. They also went on to explain that Bobby Moore, Geoff Hurst and Martin Peters; who all played for West Ham United, had won the World Cup for England in 1966 virtually on their own. I started to look out for West Ham in the football results being read out by Dickie Davis at the end of 'World of Sport', I also wrote down all the results at the back of the Saturday edition of the Daily Express so my mum could check them against her lines in the football pools. It might seem strange but I liked the look of the name West Ham, I read the match reports on the back pages of my mum's Sunday Express and cut out any pictures of Geoff Hurst for my home made album about West Ham United.

On Saturday 7 November 1970 Mr Miller and his son Gary, who also lived in Hall Road, Fordham, sealed my life long love and passion for what I now considered 'My Football

Club'. He took the pair of us to Portman Road so we could watch Ipswich Town versus West Ham United; Gary and I sat on the old leather bench seat in the front of his dad's blue Austin A55 van. The excitement was unbearable, I was going to a live First Division football match and I would get to see the likes of Geoff Hurst, Peter Grotier and Harry Redknapp play for the very first time. It took me a long time to get to sleep the night before the match and in the morning I put on a pair of claret and blue football socks and pulled them over the top of my corduroy trouser legs. I also wore a claret and blue bobble hat and scarf my mum had bought for me and I carried a wooden rattle that I had rather clumsily painted in nearly the right club colours; I think it was nearer to fuchsia and turquoise than claret and blue. I felt really great, but in reality I probably looked a right twat.

I remember walking up the road in Ipswich towards the football ground after Mr Miller had parked his van, and we were joined by thousands of other supporters all wearing my football teams colours on their own scarves. Mr Miller paid for me to get into the ground so I used the money my mother gave me to buy a West Ham United rosette from outside the ground before we went into the stadium. Thirty-eight years later I still have that rosette and will never part with it for love nor money. We were half way up in the stand (not a seat to be seen anywhere) directly behind one of the goals; I was impressed with the view of the green pitch and the sheer volume of noise from the West Ham fans singing 'I'm forever blowing bubbles', they drowned out any sound coming from the Ipswich fans. The song confused me somewhat as I had no idea what blowing bubbles had to do with the game of football, but by the end of the game I knew all the words and drove my mother to distraction for weeks afterwards as I sang it over and over again.

The noise from my fellow supporters was deafening as the players came out of the left hand corner of the ground and onto the pitch, I saw Geoff Hurst, an English World Cup winning hero for the first time in my life. It felt like watching the entrance of my favourite gladiator into the coliseum in Rome. I liked the colours of the West Ham kit but when I saw the team wearing them on that day, I fell in love with them. We lost the game 2 – 1 in the end but I saw Geoff Hurst score a goal at our end of the ground, it was a day that has remained permanently etched in my brain.

The Clacy Clan moved to Chelmsford about six months later so my dad didn't have so far to drive to work and I never saw Gary or Mr Miller ever again. They gave me a football club that I have continued to love and support for over forty years, but some Saturday afternoons Mr Miller, I curse the very day I met you and your son.

HOW MUCH TO BUY YOUR SISTER

Not only was my sister Susan a very good student who enjoyed academia even more than I enjoyed a Curly Wurly, she was also a very pretty girl who was popular with both her teachers and peers at Stanway Secondary Modern School. I, on the other hand, was both plain butt ugly and just seemed to annoy everyone I met, including all my Teachers and peers at Stanway Secondary Modern School.

Now, Stephen Mortlock was about the same age as my sister and he lived at the end of the Cul de Sac in Hall Road a few doors down from our house. He was tall for his age and wore glasses that made him look a bit of a geek. His father who managed a pig farm that was a couple of miles North of Fordham village bore a striking resemblance to Ron Ely, the actor who played Tarzan in the 1960s TV series. Stephen, David Parker and I used to help his dad on the farm during the Summer Holidays, we would feed the pigs, stack bales of hay and have some of the best ever play fights in the farms hayloft. I liked Stephen Mortlock because he was more grown up and intelligent than me (in reality, probably everyone was more grown up and intelligent than me); I suppose I looked upon him as a surrogate older brother. He also had the best collection of Tommy Gunn (alter ego to Action Man) soldiers and equipment, in his two older brother's bedroom was a wall frame holding a massive collection of beautifully assembled and painted Airfix model aircraft. Added to these facts; they also had a life size carved wooden copy of the British Army's 7.62mm Self Loading Rifle and a working candy floss machine in their garage, in my opinion they were definitely the luckiest family in the world. I often begged Mrs Mortlock to let me live with them.

Whilst playing in his sitting room one day I felt Stephen wasn't giving our latest battle his full attention, as my Action Man bayoneted his Tommy Gunn in the neck his mind seemed to be elsewhere:

Me: "You're dead."

Stephen: "She's alright your sister Susan, I quite like her."

Me: "What?"

Stephen: "I think your sister Susan is quite nice."

Me: "You know she's a girl, don't you."

Stephen: "Yeah, but she's quite nice for a girl. Do you think she will go out with me?"

Me: "You know she can't play football don't you."

Stephen: I don't want to play football with her; I want to take her out to the pictures, if you can get her to go out with me I'll give you all my Tommy Gunn stuff."

Me: "Bloody hell, you would give me all this stuff just for the loan of my sister?"

Stephen: "Only if she will go out with me."

Me: "Let's say Susan won't go out with you, will Trisha my other sister do as a replacement."

Stephen: "No way, she is one frightening specimen."

I couldn't believe my luck, two Tommy Gunn's, loads of weapons and other equipment just to borrow my sister; I didn't have a clue what he wanted to take my sister to the pictures for, she probably wouldn't even enjoy the film 'The Green Berets', one way or another I had to get her to agree though. The only problem when dealing with sisters is the fact that they often don't see the bigger picture. I had to be cautious as I questioned her about Stephen's chances of making her the new Mrs Susan Mortlock. A lot was at stake.

Me: "Sue…do you like Stephen Mortlock?"

Sue: "He's alright…why?"

Me: "He likes you and wants to take you to the pictures."

Sue: "Well why hasn't he asked me out then."

Me: "I think he's a bit shy."

The silence was palpable as Sue concentrated on her homework.

Me: "Well… do you want to go out with him or not, I need an answer."

Sue: "What's it got to do with you if I go out with him or not."

Me: "He said I could have all his Tommy Gunn stuff if you go out to the pictures with him…please go out with him."

Sue: "No, bugger off will you; I'm trying to do my geography homework. Hey, before you go, you wouldn't happen to know which State in America has a more suitable climate for growing citrus fruits would you? Is it California or Maine?"

She might as well have asked me to explain Einstein's theory of relativity. The deal was off; there was no way Susan was going to prostitute herself for some action figures, even though they came with all that extra equipment and weapons. The most annoying thing about this whole sorry affair was that Susan changed her mind a couple of weeks later, typical bloody female, she went out with Stephen after he gathered up the courage to ask her himself. The bastard didn't give me his Tommy Gunn stuff either.

A BIT OF A SLIP UP

The Clacy home was run more like an army unit than the warm loving family environment that it could have been, and it wasn't due to my fathers' life long service in the British Army and Civilian Prison Service. No, I'm afraid the rigours of our childhood were down to our mum, she told us, "There are four of you and I don't have the time or inclination to pander to everyone's needs, it is therefore a case of all hands to the pump."

My mum cooked the distressed and meagre ingredients that went into our very basic meals and we children were assigned all the kitchen fatigues, Trisha, the eldest in the Clacy brood had to wash up the dishes, Susan had to dry up the dishes and I had to put everything away as well as clearing the dining table. Yes that's right, muggins here got two jobs. David, the youngest in the Clacy Clan got away with doing nothing because he was only four years old but in my eyes he was just a lazy bastard. After every Sunday dinner he just sat on mums lap and watched the Sunday afternoon film on TV in the front room as we slaved away out in the kitchen. Whenever dad was at work in one of Her Majesty's Prisons, his meal would be dished up and placed on a plate over a saucepan of water ready to be heated up when he returned to his and our utopia. There were times when he came home late from keeping the nation safe from all those murderers and rapists and found his wonderful family watching the Morecambe and Wise show on the box in the corner of the room. Not one of us even acknowledged he had come in from work as we continued to watch the TV. Mum would shout, "John! Your dinners on the stove" and we would remain seated and continue with our impression of the Royle family having a really, really, really lazy day. Dad usually ate his meals alone in the dining room.

As children we also had to iron our own school uniforms from the age of seven upwards and God help anyone if mum found an unmade bed after we had departed the barracks for school. It wasn't all doom and gloom though, I remember one Sunday afternoon my siblings and I were cleaning up the kitchen as mum and the lazy little bastard watched TV, Susan made Trisha and I laugh as she slipped on some water on the floor and fell on her bum. As Trisha and I snorted helplessly at Susan, she decided to squirt some washing up liquid on the floor and we all pretended to ice skate and noisily bumped into the kitchen cupboards. I can remember shrieking with laughter as we bumped into each other and kept slipping and sliding all over the place. We made a bit too much noise though and disturbed mums' and the little bastards' afternoon entertainment, she came storming into the kitchen to sort us out and shouted, "You noisy bloody kids are going to get it in a minute!" It was at this moment that my life went into a slow motion action replay; I can still remember the frame-by-frame drama of my mums' legs flying up in the air and disappearing over her head as she slipped on some washing up liquid. The image and sound of her flying through the air and landing on her back will stay with me until the day I die. Poor old mum landed on her back with a sickening thud and she had the wind knocked right out of her. There followed a couple of seconds silence as we stood, open mouthed, looking down at our very undignified mother gasping for breath, she looked like a recently caught and laid out trout on the river bank that was struggling to breath. Unfortunately I was the one that broke the silence and I guffawed at my mums' comical Charlie

Chaplin style antics, frighteningly, my laughter opened Pandora's Box and as I was the one to laugh the loudest, mum vented her anger on me. After struggling to her feet she lashed out at me with a wooden spoon and hit me across my buttocks, it hurt like crazy and because mum hit me so hard the spoon snapped in half and flew into the air, bizarrely this made me laugh even louder, so much so that I became hysterical and actually cried with laughter and pain. Trisha and Susan nervously joined in the laughter, firstly, because of the joy of not being the one getting a right pasting, and secondly, the sheer joy of seeing their brother take one for the team.

That was well over forty years ago and the experience stood me in good stead for when I joined the British Army where I took quite a few pastings from quite a few soldiers, but none of them were as tough as my old mum.

BULLSEYE

My younger brother David was a little shit! When I was 13 years old he had just entered his eighth, and what could easily have been his last year on this planet. We had moved from Fordham and were now living in an old semi-detached house in Broomfield just outside Chelmsford in Essex, and at every opportunity David set out to annoy me by speaking and breathing. On this particular occasion I was going out to play football with my friend Dean Ketley and the annoying little sod that my parents had lumbered me with wanted to come along as well. I considered my brother to be a miniature version of 'Dopey' out of 'Snow White and the Seven Dwarfs', some octogenarian ladies might have considered him cute enough but he was just a lead weight around my neck when I wanted to go out with my mates.

When I refused him permission to come over to Brooklands football pitch with us, he took the hump and kicked me up the arse as I looked under the bed for my West Ham football shirt. He took off like a startled hare out of our bedroom and onto the landing, he might have been built like a pygmy but he was fast. I scrambled to my feet to try and get my hands round his neck and I automatically grabbed one of the darts in the dart board hanging on the back of our bedroom door. Don't ask me why; it was purely an instinctive reaction to my humiliating arse kicking by the bantamweight baby of the family. Clutching my brass spear I sped out onto the landing and turned right to see David fleeing down the stairs, he had to negotiate a ninety degree right turn half way down the stairs; and at the bottom he would have to do a complete U turn into the hall to get out of the house through the back door. He might have been fast but the turns would slow him down and I could close in on my prey, I wanted to avenge the horrendous shame he had heaped upon me. As David got to the bottom of the stairs and started his U turn, I realised I was losing ground and the little bastard just might escape my legitimate punishment.

After cornering the ninety degree bend on the stairs I leaned over the banister on my right hand side and drew back the arm of justice; and I let fly with the missile that would restore the equilibrium of life. As the dart, complete with a green plastic flight, hurtled towards my brothers' forehead, I was suddenly awash with feelings of regret; perhaps this wasn't a good idea. The dart struck David in the centre of his head just above the hairline and he seemed to yelp like the mangy dog he was. His forward motion and the pain in his head seemed to make him spin round and collapse onto his back; his eyes were closed and he remained motionless. It appeared that I had in fact killed my brother; I couldn't see any court in the land agreeing with my plea of not guilty due to the fact that "My brother often got right on my tits". As I stared down at my recently deceased sibling I thought, 'If mum finds out about this she'll go mad'.

I ran down into the hallway and looked down at my lifeless brothers' cadaver; he looked like a comical unicorn with that dart sticking out of his head. As panic started to set in I knelt down, grabbed his shoulders and tried to shake him back to life by shouting, "David…David…for fucks sake David, are you alright?" David opened his eyes and sat up, the little twat then laughed in my face and shouted, "Ha Hah, you swore and I'm going to tell mum." I was so tempted to try and push that dart through his fucking skull and out the back of his infuriating head. I straddled David's puny chest and pinned his arms down at his sides, "Right you little bugger, you thought that was funny did you, well let's see if you laugh as much during the Jungle Treatment." A look of horror crossed David's face, "Please God no, not the Jungle Treatment, I can stand anything but the Jungle Treatment. I'll never do anything ever again, please let me go and I won't tell mum that you swore." My blood was up and I wanted revenge, I pulled up David's tee shirt and told him, "You're not getting away with it that easily. Oh no David…look out, the ants are coming!" At this point I started to pinch the skin on David's underdeveloped chest and left him with very distinctive weal marks, I ascertained David wasn't enjoying the attention I was lavishing on him by the awful amount of noise he was making, he screamed like an eight year old school-girl in a dark cellar. The Treatment continued onto the next phase. "Oh no David, look out, here come the lion's, lets hope they haven't got their claws out!" The scratch marks from my fingernails made his skin look like an inaccurate version of the London Underground map. David continued to make an awful amount of noise. We were now coming to the end of the Jungle Treatment so I leaned back and shouted at David, "Oh God help you David…get out of the way quickly...for Christ's sake David get out of the way. THE ELEPHANTS ARE COMING!!" I then started to pound poor old David's chest with my fists.

It sounds like I was a bit cruel to my brother but I can assure you it was in his own vested interest and I was only trying to help him become a much better person and brother. I cared about my brother, as much as is possible to love a smaller creature from within my own siblings, I probably liked him as much as I liked my own sisters, probably more so if I think about it. To prove the point I want to tell you about an incident that happened not long after this 'accident' with the dart. David was given a bit of a pasting by a big cowardly German bullyboy who lived over the road from us and David cried about it on our mum's shoulder. I don't know why I told you he was German, that fact is irrelevant to the story other than to try and win favour with you the good British reader. Anyway, when I came home and saw my brother crying as a result of his horrendous Teutonic treatment, I decided to exact some revenge. I went over to the house where the bully lived (he was considerably bigger than me by the way) and I knocked on his front door, when the black-hearted fiend opened it; I punched him several times in the face until he fell on the hallway floor crying. I left him with no doubt as to the reason for my anger, "I am the only one allowed to beat my brother up, and don't you ever forget that!"

BETTER THAN SUBUTEO

I cannot believe that I am going to let you know the most intimate and embarrassing details of my initiation into the world of sex, I don't have much to shout about in the sexual experience department but this one had a bit of farce about it. Having said that, I have had the odd moment when I ran around a bedroom like Paulo Di Canio after he scored that great goal for West Ham United against Wimbledon. You must remember the goal, Alan Hansen said on Match of the Day, "Now that is a definite contender for Goal of the Month."

I 'lost my flower' in 1972 at the tender age of fifteen years old, at the time I was staying with my sister Trisha and her husband Pete at their Married Quarter in RAF Swanton Morley in Norfolk. All three of us had been invited to a party one night by a couple that lived just a couple of doors away. Trisha had the right raving hump about something or other and decided to stay at home so she could continue spitting her dummy out in private. It turned out to be quite convenient as it happened because as she was staying home she could baby-sit her own two children; Trisha went on to have seven kids one after the other. I'm not surprised my sister was slightly psychotic; I don't think she had the chance to get over her Post Natal Depression before squirting out yet another scrap of humanity. I think the time sequence of her pregnancies would indicate my Brother in Law probably got Trisha pregnant on the couch in the delivery room immediately after giving birth. It must have been embarrassing and awkward for the theatre staff as they tried to clear things up ready for the next expectant mother.

Because of my sisters particular downwards mood swing that evening, Pete and I went round to the party without her and we were the last of the guests to arrive. The sitting room was packed with off duty RAF Servicemen and their wives and they all seemed to be slightly inebriated, we had a couple of beers from a Party Seven tin thrust at us and we did our best to try and catch up with them. The hostess of the party put on the record 'Young Girl' by Gary Puckett and the Union Gap and I noticed a bloke sat on the sofa falling asleep; he wasn't just asleep, he was pissed out of his tiny skull. Guests at the party were dancing in a cleared space that was normally used as the dining room. I looked around the room and noticed a very slim and attractive woman in her late thirties, she was dancing with a tubby balding RAF twat who obviously had no control of his legs, well, if you had control of your legs you wouldn't fucking dance like he was. The attractive woman I was eyeing up had shoulder length black hair that curled up at the end and she was wearing a very short suede dress; it had a large zip down the front so that the dress could be unzipped down to her navel when taking it off. I know I wanted her to take it off! She also had a fantastic pair of legs that seemed to stretch all the way up to her rather gorgeous arse. Not like some of the other women at the party, their arses seemed to have sagged down to the back of their knees.

The attractive woman noticed I was looking at her and came over after finishing her dance with the tubby balding twat; this sweating tub of lard would definitely have won a George Formby fancy dress competition. As she came up to me she asked if I had any cigarettes; I took out my crushed packet of unfiltered Park Drive fags and tried to look nonchalant and twenty-five years old; as I lit her one of my fags I noticed it had a 45-degree bend in it. She seemed to be impressed that I had chosen 'Trained Killer in the British Army' as a career option and asked me if I wanted to dance? Did a bear shit in the woods? We danced to 'Telegram Sam' belted out by T Rex before someone put on the record 'Puppy Love' sung by Donny Osmond; she said that she thought Donny was, "a handsome sexy young man." Now, Donny and I fortunately share the same birthday on the 7th December 1957, I therefore automatically assumed she thought I was a handsome sexy young man as well. You have to be a fifteen- year-old teenager with a rock hard erection in your pocket to understand how I came to this conclusion. Anyway, as we slowly danced to 'Puppy Love', the irony of the situation was completely lost on me; I could only concentrate on the smell of her perfume and the feel of her warm body slowly gyrating against mine.

It was getting late and the women at the party had decided to start de-bagging some of the men and my Brother in Law was next in line. They threw his trousers out of the sitting room window and he had to go outside to find them. I went upstairs to empty my bladder and after coming out of the toilet I just happened to bump into my attractive and sexy new friend who had been waiting for me on the landing. She said, "Hi, I've been looking for you". She then moved towards me and put her arms round my waist and gently squeezed my firm young buttocks (Oh how I remember those days of firm buttocks). It took a nanosecond to realize that her very energetic hot wet tongue was causing the tickling sensation at the back of my throat. My initial thought was 'Fucking hell, this is better than Subutteo'. I asked about her husband and she explained he was the drunk snoring on the sofa, she then asked if I would escort her safely home to number 13 just up the road. That bear was still taking a very large dump in the woods. Whoever said the number 13 was an unlucky number clearly didn't know what they were talking about. It was at this point my now re-trousered Brother-in-Law appeared at the bottom of the stairs and shouted, "Come on, were going home. I'm on duty tomorrow!" Of all the houses on that estate, my attractive and sexy new friend had to live at number fucking 13. My brain and genitals both screamed, "Noooooooo, you have to be kidding us. Tell him you'll be home later; go on tell him, you're not in the fucking RAF. This is your time now; you need to plunge this aching lead pipe into something wet and warm, go on, tell him to fuck off." Pete was having none of it and he demanded that we went home immediately and unfortunately that was what we did.

In the morning Trisha seemed to be even angrier than she was the night before, it might have had something to do with the fact that I told her about Pete getting de-bagged at the party, he might have spoiled my night but I made sure his life was going to be a misery for the next few weeks. After Pete had gone to work with a rather large flea in his ear, Trisha asked me to nip round to the families NAAFI to buy a loaf of bread. I took the long way round to the NAAFI, which meant I would have to walk past number 13 where my snogging partner from the previous evening lived. I say the long way round; in fact it was in completely the opposite direction to the NAAFI. I knocked on the front door and lamely asked if she wanted anything from the NAAFI as I was going for a loaf of bread for my big and mentally unstable sister. Naively I couldn't believe she fell for my pathetic excuse for calling and she invited me in for a moment as the weather was poor and she was feeling the cold through her skimpy negligee. Actually I ended up staying for an hour; don't get me wrong; I'm not saying my sexual prowess was so good that I lasted an hour the first time we did it, the first act of love was over and done with in a very short time but my seducer encouraged me to "Have another go dear". My femme fatale seemed to be fascinated by my young body and she was happy for me to stay for another round of bumping uglies. It was up to that time probably the singularly best hour of my life. I walked into house number 13 a handsome sexy young man and came out a gibbering bowl of jelly; I had an inane grin on my face that even the Gestapo couldn't have removed. What I had just been through (pardon the pun) was even better than Subutteo and snogging put together; needless to say I didn't try to phone Esther Rantzen to make an official complaint.

I skipped back to my sisters' gaff and the smile was quickly wiped off my face as the front door was wrenched open and I came face to face with a very angry sister doing her impression of the Mad Woman from Borneo. "Where the bloody hell have you been, and where is the bread!" I felt it probably wasn't a good time to share my wonderful news with Trisha because she seemed to be in yet another very unreasonable mood, so I apologised and headed up to the NAAFI taking the short route.

IT'S AN ARMY LIFE FOR ME

In my final year at Broomfield Secondary Modern School I had my first interview with a careers officer, we had our meeting in a small office near the schools large foyer and he asked me what I wanted to do in my future employment. I was surrounded by an abundance of lever arch files and leaflets that had all sorts of information about different jobs that could provide me with a possible future livelihood. I didn't have to read any information though; the only thing I was interested in was the large posters on the wall that had been provided by Chelmsford's Army Careers Information Office. There were pictures of all sorts of soldiers in combat uniforms carrying all sorts of weaponry, and those that were in civilian clothing were off duty and either standing in a Hong Kong bar chatting up a good looking army nurse, or they were skiing down a snow covered mountain on a beautiful sunny day. That was the sort of career I wanted; looking hard and trying to get into the knickers of a QARANC (Queen Alexandra Royal Army Nursing Corps); she didn't need to be that good looking either because I had hit a dry spell since losing my virginity. My careers officer and I had the following conversation:

Careers officer: "Right Brian, have you had any thoughts about what you want to do when you leave school."

Me: "Yes. I want to join the army."

Careers Officer: "Hmm, ok, that is a possibility, but it might not be quite how you think it is in the army. It can be a tough life you know. Have you thought about some other options?"

Me: "No. I want to join the army."

Careers Officer: "Yes I understand that Brian, but as I have explained to you, life in the army can be very tough, I mean, you might have to go to Northern Ireland and that could be a very distressing experience. There is more to life in the Armed Forces than skiing and wearing a smart uniform you know."

Me: "Yes, my dad has told me that life in the infantry is shit."

Careers Officer: "Oh good, I'm glad someone has at least explained the down side of a life in uniform. So, bearing that in mind, what career do you think you might like to pursue after leaving school?"

Me: "I want to join the army."

Careers Officer: "Oh my Lord give me strength… Brian, listen to me will you, I know you want to join the British Army, you've already said that, but have you even thought about a different possible profession, there are thousands of careers that don't involve you having to kill people. What about an apprenticeship in carpentry? Your woodwork teacher seems to think that if you applied yourself, you may well have a future in this vocation."

Me: "No, I just want to join the army."

Careers Officer: "YES! I KNOW YOU WANT TO JOIN THE BLOODY ARMY!!!! Sorry…I'm really sorry for raising my voice Brian but listen to what I'm saying to you,… you may not be able to pass all the mental and physical tests to gain entrance to the army, you really should try to think of some other occupation or trade just in case you don't like it in the army and you want to leave. There must be something else you might like to do other than joining the army, just think about it for a couple of minutes and we can explore any other possibilities."

Me: Ummm….ok, if I can't get into the army, I think I want to join the Royal Air Force."

Careers Officer: "Oh my God! I tell you what, just fuck off and join the army then."

AS A SOLDIER

As a soldier, well quite frankly, I was an 'also ran'. I was just about average at everything I did in the army, on a Basic Fitness Test, which is a three-mile run; I always came in under the required time but usually finished in the middle of the pack. I was a good HGV Driver and passed all my driving tests without any dramas, the same applied to all the other courses I had to go on, but I never came in first on anything. That included any fitness training, shooting competitions, NBC (Nuclear Biological and Chemical Warfare) training and all the other shit we had to do in the British Army.

I was an 'also ran' like the majority of soldiers, we liked the fact that women were attracted to the uniform and we had the best mates in the world to go on the piss with, but when it came to being serious about soldiering, the majority of us in the British Army were definitely found wanting. But if you think about it, we were the normal ones. Any soldier who wanted to push his way through all sorts of pain barriers just to obtain a different coloured hat, well, the bloke was a knob as far as we were concerned. Once these competitive and dedicated soldiers had won either a maroon, green or sand coloured beret, they had to continue with a life of pain, misery and discomfort just to prove what a magnificent military specimen they were. We 'also ran' soldiers on the other hand did our very best to get out of strenuous exercise, guard duties and anything else that was of no interest, or of any benefit to us personally. We weren't knobs, we were the switched on squaddies.

So, that was the sort of soldier I was throughout my inglorious and undistinguished military career, I do admit to being proud of the fact that I did complete two tours of duty in Northern Ireland as an RCT Driver with 10 Regiment RCT. My first tour was in Belfast with 9 Squadron RCT and the second was in South Armagh with 17 Squadron RCT where I sustained a head injury one night whilst working in a VCP (vehicle Check Point) on the Dublin Road just outside Newry. As a result of this incident I became an insulin dependent diabetic, but you can read all about that in 'Harry was a Crap Hat'. After working as a Regimental Medical Assistant in 66 Squadron RCT for a couple of years, I had to transfer to the Royal Army Dental Corps if I wanted to continue with a career in the British Army. The law states that Insulin Dependant Diabetics cannot drive Heavy Goods Vehicles and the Regimental Medical Assistant job wasn't considered a permanent profession within the ranks of the RCT. Therefore I became a 'Gob Doctor', which in short meant I was a dental nurse who could do a bit of typing. I did tell you my life in the army was an inglorious and undistinguished one. I served in the ranks of the RADC in BAOR (British Army of the Rhine) and the UK until I reached the rank of Sergeant; anyway, that is the gist of it. The following sequential anecdotes will expand on my stories in 'Harry was a Crap Hat' and about my life as a soldier.

OATH OF ALLEGIANCE

The Recruiter in Chelmsford's Army Recruiting Office was a Warrant Officer Class 2 from the Queens Regiment; he was a loud, barrel chested and intimidating man. He wore his Number 2 Service Dress uniform like a badge of honour; he had all the right accoutrement's with it as well. Across his ample chest he wore a wide red sash that had a large tassel, which ended at his left hip, and above his left breast pocket he wore some medal ribbons, one of which was a Military Medal for gallantry. Not only was this man a proper soldier, he was also a certified war hero.

When he asked me what I wanted to do in the army I told him I fancied being a Royal Military Policeman, they looked very smart and obviously got to order blokes around whilst wearing a pretty red hat. My recruiting Warrant Officer was just like my careers officer at Broomfield School, he tried to put me off what I knew I wanted to do, but this experienced soldier clearly knew what he was talking about and didn't pull any punches. "So you want to become a Military Policeman do you? Imagine if you can, getting the shit kicked out of you almost every night of your service career by soldiers of every army around the world." He pointed to a poster on the wall that displayed the cap badges of every Regiment and Corps within the British Army, "Any soldier wearing any of those cap badges will take the greatest of pleasure in laughing at you behind your back, and when tanked up with alcohol they will all want to separate your head from the rest of your body. Not even the Royal Military Police like the Royal Military Police. Do yourself a favour son and choose something else." He tried to coerce me into joining the Royal Army Ordnance Corps as a store-man but I wasn't having any of that, I didn't want to stack blankets for a living. My Brother in law was a driver in the Royal Air Force and I fancied driving big trucks and ambulances like he did. A deal was struck between the two of us and he allowed me to join the Royal Corps of Transport, I say allowed because army recruiters will only let you do what they want you to do.

The recruiter was now about to give me a days pay and all I had to do was swear an oath of allegiance to the Queen whilst placing my hand on a bible and the Union flag of Great Britain. That's all I had to do, but that would have been too simple for me, no, I had to go and upset the apple cart by annoying my recruiter who seemed to think that the oath of allegiance was something every soldier has to embody within their very heart. I can imagine when he took his oath of allegiance that he had it tattooed on his foreskin so he would never forget it; the Oath of Allegiance was something incorporated within his body and soul. The oath went along these lines:

"I Brian John Clacy swear by almighty God that I will be faithful and bear true allegiance to Her Majesty Queen Elizabeth the Second, Her heirs and successors and that I will as in duty bound honestly and faithfully defend Her Majesty, Her heirs and successors in Person, Crown and dignity against all enemies and will observe and obey all orders of Her Majesty, Her heirs and successors and of the Generals and Officers set over me."

That's all I had to say and I would have a foot in the British Army's front door, my recruiter didn't want to hear me question this oath or start to take it apart to try and interpret every single sentence. I mean, what was all that bit about 'obey all orders' and 'Her Heirs and successors', I didn't mind doing what the queen and the odd General asked me to do but I wasn't going to run around after everyone. It was all a bit of lighthearted banter really but the old soldier didn't see it that way and he told me so through gritted teeth, "If you don't believe in this oath then walk out of that door right now, I want you to grow up and stop pissing me around, make up your mind what it is you want to do." I was totally contrite and apologised for messing him about, he then said through gritted teeth, "Good! Now take the fucking oath and mean it!"

A ROYAL VISIT

Any Junior Leaders, from any branch of the Junior British Army, who weren't involved in any specific training at a given moment, could be released to other units to provide temporary manpower. About half way through my training I was sent to Tidworth Garrison to provide some additional manpower for the annual Garrison Point to Point competition. In all there were ten Junior Drivers from Taunton and we were attached to the local Donkey Walloping (Cavalry) unit; we were instructed to help out with any general duties they wanted us to complete. The local Donkey Wallopers were organising and administrating the competition because they, and other Donkey Walloping Regiments; were the only units that were involved in this sort of horsey set crap, they were very serious about getting everything just right because the usual Royal Rabble would be attending, I would be involved in another point to point in a medical capacity later on in my career (see Lieutenant Colonel Bell RAMC). As far as the horsy lot (I think it was the 17/21 Lancers) were concerned, we Troggs were treated as their insignificant labourers.

On the day before the competition started; my comrades in arms and I were pounding some six sided wooden stakes into the grass area near the edge of the competition course, we had to beat the posts into the ground using a 9lb sledgehammer whilst keeping our head and fingers out of the way. It was hot and frustrating work in the mid-summer heat. Once the posts were evenly spaced out across the area they were painted white and connected by a long and pristine white nylon rope. These ropes would hopefully stop any spectators from walking into the path of a charging horse and rider in the competition. One of my RCT comrades on the day was a Cumbrian lad called Junior Driver Biggins; this Northern Neanderthal had the manners, intelligence and social graces of the violent punk rocker Vyvyan out of the 1980s TV comedy series 'The Young Ones'. 'Biggy' was a big lad and a hard grafter, he swung the 9lb sledgehammer around like most people use a newspaper to swat flies, he sweated his bollocks off as he pounded stake after stake into the ground.

As he was putting the final touches to his hammering masterpiece, a woman riding a beautiful chestnut brown horse rode up to where we were working and politely asked, "Hello chaps, what are you doing here?" 'Biggy', breathing quite heavily because of his over exertion with the 9lb lumpy hammer, took the time to stop, wipe the sweat from his forehead and replied, "What the fuck does it look like we're doing, we're putting up this rope to stop you and your idiotic mates from riding up to where you and your horse are now standing, have you got any other fucking daft questions?"

Her Royal Highness Princess Anne roared with laughter and rode off.

CAPTAIN McCLOUD SAS

Driver's serving in the Royal Corps of Transport were a tough breed of soldier; they drank hard, played hard and fought hard. But when it came to the tactical side of soldiering we were usually found wanting, as a unit we would take on any Airborne or Marine soldiers in a pub fight, and we could possibly take as many scalps as we lost. But put us out in the field to make use of our soldiering skills, for instance, noise and light discipline, camouflage, and Infantry Battle Skills, most footsloggers would run rings around us. We trade soldiers' had a grounding in infantry techniques, but RCT Driver's spent more time in training on vehicle maintenance and driving proficiency than on infantry tactics and battle skills. Every soldier in the British Army learns the basics of how to fight and survive as an Infantry soldier, (all personnel in the British Army are a soldier first and a tradesman second) but they also have to learn about their own trade, which takes up a lot of trade training time. It takes a long time to learn the skills of an Infantryman, which is a trade in itself.

In the latter stages of my training at the Junior Leaders Regiment RCT in Taunton, I was a member of Senior Troop and we were taking part in an infantry role Exercise out on the Quantock Hills. We were sent out in squads of about ten men to attack and defend each other's bivouac areas. My squad were going to do a night attack on another squad who were dug in a couple of miles from our own area. I was tail end Charlie as we tramped rather noisily in the direction of our pretend enemies. Noise travels a long distance at night, which is why noise and light discipline is so important when trying to sneak up and attack an enemy position. Soldiers on patrol should also maintain about ten meters distance from the soldier in front in case of being ambushed or someone standing on an explosive mine, it lessens the chance of sustaining multiple casualties from one explosion. Having said that, soldiers are no different from the average civilian when it comes to being frightened of the bogey man, they will bunch up on patrol to get that feeling of security from standing close to a friend. You just never know who or what is out there in the dark, and whatever it is, it just might jump out on you.

I could hear one of the two soldiers ahead of me fart rather loudly and they both giggled like a couple of schoolgirls, this was audibly very clear to me even though they were whispering and I was about the regulation ten meters behind them. As the patrol continued my mind started to wander as I thought about Sue from Legs and Co on Top of the Pops (when bored, soldiers minds usually turn towards sex or mischief), I was imagining what she would do to me sexually after I had saved her life and carried her out of a burning building. I was at the point in my fantasy where I was copping a feel from a very grateful Sue when someone charged at me from behind, whoever my assailant was they silently grabbed me, covered my mouth and nose, lifted me off the ground and bundled me into a ditch just to the side of the track our patrol was wandering along. I was held face down like a British Prime Minister in his First year at Eton, my attacker used his full body weight to restrain me, and I could neither shout nor move in any way shape or form. My patrol comrades never heard a sound and continued on their way completely oblivious to me being attacked. The bloke holding me down leaned in towards my left ear and whispered, "Driver Clacy, this is Captain McCloud speaking, as far as your patrol is concerned you are now dead, don't make any sound or movement. Do you understand?" Captain McCloud had been serving with the SAS (Special Air Service Regiment) and had come to the Royal Corps of Transport after completing his tour of duty with them; if I remember correctly he was now the Officer Commanding Senior Troop.

I nodded that I understood who he was and that I would comply with his instructions, my heart was going at the rate of an express train. He again leaned into my left ear and said, "Do you want to be on my side now?" Fucking right I wanted to be on his side, this fighting enigma and I were about to make up a formidable fighting military machine. After allowing me to stand up he again whispered in my ear, "Have you got one up the spout?" He was enquiring as to whether or not I had cocked my SLR and had put a blank round into the chamber ready to fire the weapon. I hadn't. He went on, "You should always cock your weapon and put your safety catch on before going out on a fighting patrol Driver Clacy, if you have to cock it prior to an ambush at night, the enemy will hear you and have a split second to kill you before you have the chance to kill him. Very quietly put one up the spout and make sure your safety catch is on, ok, now follow me." He quickly set off on a tangent direction to where my previous patrol comrades were heading and I moved as quickly and silently as I could to keep up with him. After about 5 minutes we came to a clearing and in the bright moonlight I saw a track that was about fifteen meters away from us, Captain McCloud put his hand up to indicate that he wanted me to stop, he then motioned me to lie down on the wet grass next to him. Again he leaned into my left ear and whispered, "Your mates will be coming along this track from the right hand side and this will be our killing zone, when the Patrol Commander gets level with that bush over there, I will start killing them from left to right, when you hear me fire my first shot I want you to start taking out all hostile targets from the tail end Charlie in towards the middle of the patrol. Do you understand Driver Clacy?" I began to worry about Captain McCloud's grip on reality; he actually used the words 'kill' and 'take out hostile targets' and 'killing zone', I began to wonder if we were actually going to eliminate all my mates. This was one scary fucking bloke and he seemed to be taking all this a bit too seriously for my liking.

I could hear the patrol approaching long before I could see them, two of the blokes had lit cigarettes which I could clearly see as they took a puff and they seemed to be making an awful racket but they probably thought they were being as quiet as church mice. As the first guy got level with the bush, 'the boss' opened fire with his blank ammunition and made me jump out of my skin; I then started blatting off my full magazine of blank rounds. The patrol stood around in the killing zone in total confusion and if this was a real ambush we could easily have killed them all.

Captain McCloud stood up after we had emptied our magazines and shouted at the patrol, "You are all dead, Driver Clacy and I have wiped out your complete Section, you two at the back haven't even noticed that Driver Clacy is no longer at the end of your patrol." He then conducted a complete and improvised lesson on everything they had done wrong, how you should always keep an eye on the bloke behind you, noise discipline, no smoking whilst out on patrol, putting one up the spout and what to do in the event of being ambushed. I stood to one side of my comrades and nodded in agreement at 'the bosses' comments, I felt so superior to them because I hadn't been ambushed, I was one of the ambushers.

We continued with the patrol after Captain McCloud had disappeared into the night like some mysterious super hero, in true RCT style we never found the other section, and they never found us either.

HANNAH GORDEN'S BOTTOM

I was lucky enough to be selected to help out at the Dunhill Horse of the Year Show in 1974, from what I remember, myself and thirty other RCT Junior Leaders from Taunton were sent on attachment to Earls Court in London. Captain Morrison RCT and Sergeant (Voodoo) Davies RCT, Morley Troops' Sergeant, were put in charge of us for the two weeks we were based in the capital. Yes, Sergeant Davis was from an Afro-Caribbean background, and no I am not a racist, whilst at Taunton this amazing sergeant was always referred to as 'old Voodoo', but never to his face. We afforded him too much respect as a Senior Non Commissioned Officer to take those sort of liberties, he knew he was called voodoo and he played up to the name, he had a large knobbly stick on his desk that he claimed had magical powers. He threatened that any Junior Leader who brought bad vibes into his office would be put under a spell.

On arrival at the Earls Court Arena we were allocated some rooms on the walkway situated above and around the arena; we then dumped our kitbags, set up our camp beds and laid out our sleeping bags. We were then introduced to Mr Alan Ball who was the organiser/designer of the jumps out in the arena. He took Sergeant Davis over to one corner of the display arena and told him that would be his command and control point, we would all have to report to Sergeant Davis at that specific location for any instructions that were to be dished out. Two Junior Leaders were allocated to each jump and whilst a horse and rider were competing we had to remain behind the arena wall. Each jump consisted of two wings with metal crescent shaped brackets that held three or four poles in place, if a horse caught one of the poles it would simply roll out of the bracket. If the jump or poles were knocked over we were told to wait until the rider had finished the whole course before re-assembling it ready for the next competitor. I was surprised at how heavy the poles were and stunned that a horse didn't injure itself when they caught their hooves on them as they jumped over each obstacle.

We got some practice assembling the jumps and then stood at our individual stations as some of the competitors practiced in the arena itself. The BBC was covering the whole competition on television, if I remember correctly it was viewed most evenings on BBC 1. On one particular night some old style carriages were putting on a show as they were pulled around the arena; this was added purely as an entertainment item for the crowd, it had nothing to do with the tournament competition. One of the coaches was a mail/passenger stagecoach that had been built in the early 1800's and the passengers, who waved at the crowd as it was pulled around by six big white horses; were all dressed up in old fashion clothes with top hats and bonnets. The driver of this particular coach got to the end of the arena but was travelling too fast to negotiate the u-turn at the end and the whole thing tipped over onto its left hand side. Luckily non of the women and children travelling on the coach were badly hurt, they just seemed to be a bit shaken up, twenty soldiers from the Junior Leaders Regiment RCT came to the rescue and we lifted the coach back on its wheels. The driver held onto the reins and controlled the horses as we did the hard work, one of the lads said to him, "You fucked that up mate." Sergeant Davis told the gobby Junior Leader to shut up. I noticed a famous Yorkshire show jumping hero, who shall remain nameless, was standing behind the arena wall watching the spectacle unfold, he watched us carry crying children to the first aid room and assisting the other passengers out of the coach, but he didn't move a muscle to help out at all. He eventually looked at his watch and moaned, "Tut bloody show jumping is going to be delayed because of this!" It took about twenty minutes to get everything back on track, much to the irritation of the great Yorkshire show jumping hero.

This wasn't the only drama during the two weeks at the Olympia arena, some celebrities were invited to take part in a scaled down version of the competition and one of them came a right cropper. The actress Hannah Gordon was the next celebrity to have a go round the course. At the time, Hannah was a television family favourite in the UK; she was starring alongside John Alderton in the prime-time TV series 'My wife next door'. If you aren't old enough to remember this show, do yourself a favour and Google it on your computer, my father and I were both totally in love with this beautiful woman. Hannah had negotiated several jumps and was about halfway down one side of the arena when her horse refused and she was thrown headfirst over the jump. This happened right in front of one of the BBC's television cameras. From where I was positioned I could clearly see the jump collapse, Hannah was lying motionless on her back on the soft wood chippings. Alan Ball was the first person to get to Hannah and after checking her over he shouted something to Sergeant Davis, old Voodoo in turn shouted as only a British Army Sergeant can, "Junior Driver's Clacy and Dunlop, grab this stretcher and report to Mr Ball. Come on you two, move yourselves!!!" (If a clip of this incident is ever put on You Tube; you won't be able to tell Vic Dunlop and me apart, we looked like twins. We were equally ugly).

Vic and I grabbed the stretcher and doubled over to Alan Ball, I tried so very hard to not look at the camera, I tried so very hard not to think of how much of a hero I looked, I even tried to stay focused on what we were doing, but it was all to no avail. Damn it, but I looked good. Vic Dunlop and I opened the green army stretcher and kicked in the metal bars so it that would remain open and rigid. Alan Ball looked at Vic and said, "You grab the casualty's feet, I will lift her head and shoulders, and you, (meaning me) you put your hands under her middle bit; and we will all lift at the same time and keep her spine straight. Sergeant Davis! You slide the stretcher underneath the casualty after we have lifted her." I hadn't noticed that Sergeant Davis had arrived and was watching over the whole incident, I also hadn't noticed that everyone was focused on the job in hand, and I also hadn't noticed that this whole incident was being dealt with in such a professional manner by everyone but me. Christ almighty, I was kneeling down beside Hannah fucking Gordon for Christ's sake, and not only that, I was about to cop a feel of her rather nice bottom. Life doesn't get any better than that.

I savoured the moment and looked straight at the BBC camera as I lowered Hannah onto the stretcher, after standing up; Vic Dunlop grabbed the feet end of the stretcher and I grabbed the head end, Vic lead the way as we then carried the beautiful Hannah Gordon to the first aid room. As we went through the gap in the arena wall, and in full view of the BBC camera, Valerie Singleton of Blue Peter fame came up to the stretcher and grabbed Hannah's hand and said, "Oh my God! Is she going to be alright?" Without a word of a lie, I tried to re-assure her when I said,

"Don't worry ma'am, she is in safe hands, we're professionals."

CONVOY COCK

10 Regiment RCT was known within the Corps as the unit from hell itself, every hard drinking, hard fighting, and trouble-making misfit that other RCT units didn't want, somehow ended up at 10 Regt in Bielefeld. I went straight to 10 Regt from the Junior Leaders Regiment RCT in Taunton, where I had just completed 18 months of basic training. As I went to look at the postings list on the notice board I remember thinking, 'Please God don't let me be posted to 10 Regt', we Junior Leaders who were now qualified Drivers in Senior Troop, were waiting for notification of our first posting to a working unit, we had all been warned that 10 Regt RCT in Bielefeld was the posting to avoid. I looked down the list of units to find which one had my name typed under it, I muttered the units as I looked through the lists:
"1 Squadron RCT, no."
"26 Squadron RCT, no."
"68 Squadron RCT, no."
"8 Regt RCT, no."
"10 Regt RCT, …Oh shitty death!"

Although nervous about being posted to the toughest unit in the RCT that was often referred to as a 'Penal Unit'; part of me felt proud that I was being sent to a unit where most Drivers would fear to tread. I thought, 'surely all those dreadful stories can't be true'. To a degree some of the stories were true as 10 Regt had more than its fair share of hard-men; but once you were known within the unit and could prove you wouldn't bottle it in a bar fight; they became very good friends who would look after you through thick and thin. In the early days of my time at 10 Regt I learned to keep my eyes and ears open and my big mouth shut; those that didn't follow my lead paid the price by getting a smack in the mouth.

I learned which tough guys to avoid and which ones I could trust, my first detail for 9 Squadron involved a long drive to an RAOC (Royal Army Ordnance Corps) Depot at Dulmen, and I was appointed co-driver to a Lance Corporal who was a short but very stocky man with short curly blonde hair. I really should have avoided this guy at all costs but no-one gave me any warning about his flair for exhibitionism, and when trapped in the cab of an army truck doing 100 kilometres an hour down an autobahn, it would have been impossible to avoid the following disgusting confrontation; let me explain. For the detail we were allocated an AEC 10 ton Militant, which was a diesel engined, 6x6 wheeled truck, and affectionately known by all Troggs in the Corps as a 'Millie', we had to take a full load of borrowed tentage back to the RAOC loan store. The Lance Corporal was a mean and moody type who treated me like a piece of shit, "Go and get a CES (Complete Equipment Schedule) tool-kit from the stores and stow it on the wagon, once you've done that nick a replacement indicator bulb from another 'Millie' (there was a constant shortage of vehicle bulbs in 10 Regt) and put it in our left rear indicator, report to me in the NAAFI when you've done that, I'm off for a pie and pint of milk".

On the way down to Dulmen my socially inadequate comrade hardly spoke a word to me until we were about three quarters of the way there; he turned his head slightly towards me and said, "I've got convoy cock!" To be quite honest I didn't have a clue what convoy cock was and so I smiled and just nodded saying, "Oh, right." For those who have never driven an army truck over long distances I will try to explain the phenomenon that is known in the RCT world as 'Convoy Cock'. Driving on an autobahn at 100 KPH over long distances is extremely boring and squaddie minds tend to wander when not occupied doing something mentally taxing and useful, and that wandering tends to go the way of a sexual nature. Now, if you couple that with the constant heavy vibration of the truck; the male of the species can end up with an erection in his trousers. I didn't realise this until I saw my illustrious leader unzip his denim trousers and take out what looked like a very large pink lead pipe, I noticed this large pink lead pipe had a big blue vein running up the side of it and I suddenly realized this sexual deviant had his penis in his hand and he had started to masturbate in front of me. I immediately looked out of the left hand passenger window and prayed to God asking why he had done this to me, after all, I wasn't a bad person, I wasn't exactly good but I didn't deserve to be put in this situation. I tried to not listen to his grunting and groaning by humming the Corps tune of 'Wait for the wagon". I have to admit I was a little in awe of his multi-tasking abilities and his manual dexterity, it is well known that men have often been given blow jobs whilst driving a fast flashy car; but to pull your own pud whilst driving a 10 ton truck on a busy autobahn was impressive to say the least. When the future Adolf Hitler had finished his self-relief; he flicked his messy hand out of the driver side window and said, "Ah, that's better," and we continued driving to Dulmen in complete silence. The silence didn't bother me though because I didn't want to go through a post-match discussion on how he thought he had performed and whether or not I was impressed. To those of you who doubt this story I can only assure you that it is absolutely true. I would like anyone who reads this and has gone through a similar experience to please get in contact, for no other reason than to let me know in which of Her Majesty's Prisons, this pervy bastard is safely locked up.

JUST A BIT OF SHIT

Warrant Officer Class Two SSM (Squadron Sergeant Major) Maher RCT was the toughest and most fearsome soldier I have ever met in my entire career in the British Army, in 10 Regiment RCT he was colloquially called 'The Bear', but only when out of earshot. Face to face even some of the subaltern Troop Commanders called him sir; he really did scare the shit out of everyone. This was 1976 and we army truckies in 10 Regiment RCT firmly believed that Taff Maher, and all the others Sergeant Majors in the regiment could walk on water if they wanted to. I'm not saying they were Jesus Christ incarnate; let's face it, no one in their right mind would believe that Jesus Christ could possibly inspect and terrify a whole Squadron of British Troops by himself. But Squadron Sergeant Majors could and did.

One particular Monday morning at 0800 hours I was standing next to my mate Driver Johnny Walker on 9 Squadron's Working Parade, we were waiting for 'The Bear' to inspect us and the pen pocket on the sleeve of my combat jacket had a small tear in it and it was worrying me. Any faults with our working dress would incur the wrath of this ogre of a man. As 'The Bear' inspected us one by one he would turn to Sergeant Herbert, our accompanying Troop Sergeant, and make sure he noted any faults in our dress on his clipboard. Anyone who had offended 'The Bear' with unpolished boots or having fluff on his beret was snarled at with threats of extra guard duties. He noticed the tear on my sleeve and growled in my face, "Get that fucking thing sewn up properly by the next time I see you Clacy or I'm going to shove my Pace Stick up your arse and turn you into a fucking Popsicle!" A Pace Stick is a long stick that is carried by Warrant Officers and Drill Instructors in the British Army; they are used as a symbol of authority and an aid to measuring distances on a drill square, they can also be used to point at scruffy soldiers whilst shouting obscenities. For obvious reasons the Royal Army Medical Corps recommend that soldiers avoid having a pace stick shoved up their arse, mainly because it can make marching in a smart and soldier like fashion virtually impossible; and it can also makes your eyes water. My legs were shaking as 'The Bear' and Sergeant Herbert moved on to denigrate my good friend Driver Johnny Walker.

As the Welsh Demigod looked Johnny up and down, he sneered and stuck his Pace Stick under poor old Johnny's nose and angrily spat, "There's a piece of shit on the end of my Pace Stick!" Driver Johnny Walker crossed his eyes and looked at the end of 'The Bears' Pace Stick and said, "It ain't on this end sir."

EXERCISE SPEARPOINT

This was to be my first ever NATO exercise, it was a massive war game that would involve soldiers not only from the British Army, but those from West Germany, USA, and the Netherlands. I had done a few Squadron and Regimental Exercises, but the amount of troops involved in this scheme was staggering, Germany hadn't seen this many soldiers, tanks, and trucks charging around their countryside since…well… you know. The difference in 1976 was, the Germans were now like us in the British Army, they too were the good guys, not like those dastardly fur hatted Russians on the other side of the Iron Curtain. Oh how things change with the passage of time.

I was just a small cog in this massive NATO military machine; throughout the six weeks on Exercise Spearpoint, my job in C Troop 9 Squadron RCT was to drive an AEC 10 ton Militant truck (registration number 03 FL 99). I had to drive from location to location, picking up and dumping pallets and pallets of crated simulated ammunition. Every unit in BAOR (British Army Of the Rhine) was practicing the particular role their unit would play in NATO, if the Warsaw Pact armies came out from behind that dreaded Iron Curtain and tried to seize control of Western Europe. Our brother Squadrons in 10 Regiment RCT were 17 and 36 Squadron; they were both co-located with 9 Squadron in Catterick Barracks in Bielefeld; and they were doing the same job as us on the Exercise. My particular lot in 9 Squadron were located in a large wooded area 'somewhere in Germany', I'm not getting all official secrets act on you, it was that long ago I just can't remember exactly where I was, I'm not that sure I even knew where I was back then in

1976. The following anecdote is absolutely true and the details are correct, I know this because back in 1976 I wrote an article for the 'News at Ten' (our 10 Regiment RCT monthly magazine) and I still have a copy that I've read before writing up this story.

I called the article 'The Marie Celeste of 9 Squadron' because I just disappeared off the Squadron radar on Exercise Spearpoint for nearly a week; it was a fucking fantastic but farcical week, all the time I was away from the Squadron I didn't do one guard duty, or peel any potatoes for our lazy fucking slop jockeys (regimental cooks). Whilst away from barracks all soldiers who didn't have any bird shit (rank) on their arm, were usually collared by the cooks in the field kitchen to peel the potatoes and wash all the dirty pans, this was referred to as Dixie bashing. I wouldn't mind but the fat lazy bastards of the Army Catering Corps didn't once come and help me change a punctured tyre on my 'Millie', these lazy twats didn't even do a stag on guard duty because they...Boo fucking Hoo…had to get up early to make breakfast for the Squadron, it wasn't our fault they had chosen women's work as a career choice. I shouldn't labour the point about army cooks (I'm fucking going to though) but on the BFT (Basic Fitness Test) which was a six monthly physical test that involved doing a timed three mile run, they even came in behind the REME (Royal Electrical Mechanical Engineers) Vehicle Mechanics, and the fastest VM usually came in behind the slowest RCT Driver. Apologies to my old mate Corporal Alan Scarborough REME, but you know it's true Alan.

Anyway, sorry about the ranting and raving, let's get back to Exercise Spearpoint and the tale of your intrepid hero,

Driver Harry Clacy RCT. I de-scrimmed (camouflage nets) my 'Millie' and after securing my SLR (7.62mm Self Loading Rifle) in the wagons rifle rack, I followed another truck (registration number 03FL 18) from C Troop which was driven by Driver 'Gus' Gardner and we drove out of our hide and onto the road. 'Gus' and I had been briefed in the CP (Command Post) to travel in convoy to Pombsen, which was one of the largest ammunition depots in Germany; it was located on the top of a hill in the middle of a very large wood. Pombsen was an RAOC Depot that stockpiled masses of ammunition for the British Army; they also stockpiled pallets of simulated ammunition for exercises just like Spearpoint. We had to load up our 'Millie's' with pallets of simulated 105mm artillery shells and deliver them to an XP (Exchange Point) where they would be cross loaded onto smaller 4 ton trucks for forward distribution to other locations. Once loaded up we secured our cargo with the standard issue green webbed restraining straps and then studied the BAOR road map that was issued to every Driver in the RCT. 'Gus' and I had a difference of opinion on exactly where we should be heading next, he thought we were supposed to head for an RV point in Hameln and I thought we were supposed to head back to HQ 9 Squadron RCT's hide. As 'Gus' was a couple of years older than me and a more experienced RCT soldier, I bowed to his expertise and after deliberating on which route to take we both headed off to Gordon Barracks in Hameln. About half way to our destination 'Gus' indicated and pulled over into the car park of a Gastatte on the edge of a small village, after he jumped out of his cab I saw him climb partly back into his truck to grab his 7.62mm LMG (Bren Gun to all the really old soldiers reading this), on Exercise poor old 'Gus' was always issued an LMG to cart around. After shouldering his machine-gun he walked towards my truck to obviously tell me some important details about our mission or change in plan. I wound down the window to hear what the problem was and 'Gus' said, "Have you got any money Harry because I'm fucking starving, let's get something to eat in this place." I also hadn't eaten for what seemed an eternity, so 'Gus' and I pooled what few Deutschmark's we had between us and headed into the restaurant. A rather snooty German waitress refused to serve us because we smelled of diesel and unwashed bodies, our faces were also covered in camouflage-cream (we had been on the Exercise for nearly four weeks by now), that and the fact that we were carrying firearms seemed good enough reasons for not serving us. 'Gus' on the other hand saw things differently and with the attitude of a Stormtrooper he told our hostess that we would not be leaving until we had been served some scoff, he then banged his heavy weapon on the pretty table cloth and demanded some food, "Schnell Machen"! Our hostess rather sensibly hurried out to the rear of the establishment to place our order with the chef, we couldn't have afforded to leave a tip even if we had wanted too.

I have to go off on a tangent for a moment to explain that soldiers of Her Majesty's Armed Forces in the mid 1970's were paid a paltry sum of money to keep the Warsaw Pact Military Machine at bay. After getting married I actually received a rent rebate and Family Income Supplement and I still found it hard to make ends meet, I wouldn't mind but my family and I weren't exactly living on Champagne and caviar. This was the reason why 'Gus' and I had to pool our money together to afford a relatively cheap meal. A couple of weeks earlier on Exercise Spearpoint, 'Gus' had quickly called into a branch of the Commerz Bank to write a cheque and draw some money out of his account. He locked the cab of his truck but couldn't leave a 7.62mm LMG unguarded in his vehicle, so he took it into the bank with him. With his face covered in camouflage cream and also wearing a combat uniform, he looked an intimidating figure to all the bank staff; some might say he looked like a bank robber. One of the female staff actually thought he was a bank robber and she hit the panic button next to her desk; this emergency button notified the Polizei that a raid was in progress. 'Gus' was unaware of the unfolding drama because it was a silent alarm that went straight through to the Polizei control centre. After cashing his cheque he nonchalantly walked towards the exit and was surprised, firstly, to be looking down the barrel of a German Police-officers' pistol, and secondly, to see three polizei cars with flashing blue lights on their roofs outside the bank. 'Gus' thought, 'Fuck me, some-ones in trouble'. The German Officer put his pistol away when 'Gus' explained what he was doing and produced the money and his receipt from the bank teller. Luckily all members of the German Polizei are renowned for their phenomenal sense of humour, they let him return to his truck and the Exercise after telling 'Gus' never to enter a German bank again whilst dressed as an urban terrorist and carrying a high powered firearm.

Meanwhile, after our meal of Bratwurst, Pommes frites and a couple of Herforder Pils Biers, we were much refreshed but still smelled like a couple of old tramps as we continued on our journey to Hameln. At the Royal Engineer camp in Hameln we were told, "Fuck knows why you've come here, we don't want you"! Feeling somewhat rejected 'Gus' and I put our heads together and he came up with another brilliant plan that just couldn't go wrong, "Exercise Spearpoint

Control is not far from here, let's go and ask them where we should be at this moment in time" said 'Gus' enthusiastically. To me it seemed a wonderful idea but I was just a fuckwit Driver in the Royal Corps of Transport, and if you told me to put my head in an oven I probably would have. You must bear in mind that at Exercise Spearpoint Control a Full Colonel was just a tea boy and the worst type of military vehicle in a ten-mile radius would be a posh Staff Car. The place was full to brimming with more Brigadiers and Generals than you could shake a stick at, and we were going to appear, without an invitation, in a couple of mud caked 10 ton trucks to ask, "Oy! General, can you tell us where we should be in the grand scheme of things"! The first problem we encountered at Exercise Spearpoint Control was a couple of self-opinionated monkeys (Members of the Royal Military Police Constabulary) wearing their pretty Red Caps; they were like a couple of ignoramus bouncers outside an exclusive nightclub and they refused to let us in, I wouldn't mind but we weren't even wearing trainers. 'Gus' was entering into an argument with the military law enforcers when our very own Brigade Commander, Brigadier Attack, was walking past and noticed a couple of manky 10 Regt trucks parked up at the camp entrance. Brigadier Attack was a big fan of 10 Regt RCT and all the soldiers who served within its ranks, in fact, he personally nicknamed 9 Squadron RCT as 'Shiny Nine' because he deemed us to be the best RCT Squadron in BAOR. The boys in 9 Squadron changed the name to 'Slimy Nine'. Our grey haired commander with the bushy moustache bounced into the RMP post, "Ah! 9 Squadron, what the hell are you two lads doing here"? We explained that we were lost to which the main man then ordered the monkeys to, "Give me your map for a couple of minutes, I need to show my boys where they should be heading"! One of the monkeys handed over their pristine map that was selotaped to a large wooden board, our Brig then proceeded to mess up the map by highlighting our next route with a felt tip pen. The monkeys were annoyed at the desecration of their brand new chart but could hardly raise a protestation to a Brigadier General. Once fully briefed on where we should be going, the Brigadier ushered us out of the ape house with the following warning, "You lads had better fuck off out of here smartish because the Duke of Edinburgh is arriving shortly to give this place the once over. Anyway, good luck on the rest of the Exercise and I'll see you back in Bielefeld in a couple of weeks." I thought to myself, 'I wonder if he will really give 'Gus' and I a ring after the Exercise, perhaps he might meet us for a beer in Roy's Bar over the road from 10 Regt'. Needless to say he didn't.

'Gus' and I mounted up and drove into the camp so we could turn round and head off in the direction we had been given by Brigadier Attack, as we approached the camp exit a motorcade was entering the camp with Royal and General Star insignia's all over their bumpers. It looked like the Duke and his entourage was arriving, and we departing, in the nick of time. The road was narrow but two cars could pass each other with comparative ease, but when two 10 Regt trucks were thrown into the equation other drivers should beware; the drivers of the Staff Cars really should have used a bit more discretion and common sense. RCT 10 ton truck drivers give way to no man, Royal or otherwise. With a trail of dust behind us we charged towards the exit and forced the Dukes driver to swerve off the road and drive up a grass embankment, closely followed by a couple of Staff Cars containing several VIP's. Ooops! Our two-truck convoy continued on its journey to the final frontier and after arriving 'somewhere in Germany' we parked up in a field with a multitude of other RCT wagons. 'Gus' was immediately told to leave the location and follow a convoy of Bedford RL 3 tonners, the drivers of these trucks were Mojo's, civilian drivers who wore army uniforms and were subject to military law but were never issued firearms, they were a civil service support element to the RCT.

It started to get dark and with 'Gus' now out of my life I headed off to the nearest G1098 to beg for a meal, the cooks asked which unit I was from and promptly informed me I wasn't on their Ration Role and feeding strength so I could "Go fuck myself". An 'old sweat' RCT Driver from 17 Squadron was within earshot and he came over like an avenging angel, he said, "If you don't give this lad some food I'm going to come round the other side of this table, tear off your head and have a fucking good shit down your neck. And I have to warn you I have been eating compo rations for nearly a month so it won't be a pleasant experience. Give him something to eat!!!" Discretion was the better part of valour for the 'slop jockey' and my mess tin was filled to brimming with a Baby's Head (a compo suet pudding), shit loads of instant mash and processed peas and a good covering of thick gravy. I thanked my fellow Trogg to which he just nodded, he then said out loud, "If you're here for breakfast in the morning and you get any shit from that wanker, just come and give me a shout." I was in fact there for the next four breakfasts as no-one seemed to need my load of simulated ammo, all day long I read my Sven Hassel book and went to the G1098 for breakfast, lunch, and dinner. After each meal I got back in my sleeping bag, which was laid out on the engine cover in the cab of my 'Millie' and went back to sleep. What a fan-fucking-tastic way to fight a pretend war.

About mid-morning on my fourth day in this location; the drivers' side door of my cab was wrenched open and I was awoken by the big black bushy moustache and booming voice of Corporal Dougie Allen. He was a very loud and punchy Section Commander in 9 Squadron, at 92 decibels he asked me, "Where the fuck have you been, your Troop Commander seems to think you've gone AWOL with one of his trucks, either that or you've started a mutiny somewhere"! I explained the full story and went back to sleep. Four hours later I was again woken but this time it was by my mates Driver Steve Campbell, Driver Stewart and Driver Harding, they told me they were about to leave with a convoy and would I like to re-join the Exercise and follow them to wherever they were going. I was getting a bit bored and only had a couple of chapters of my book left to read, so on my own initiative I got back into the game and followed my mates and their convoy. The Section Commander in the lead vehicle was a Corporal from A Troop in 9 Squadron and he took us down a narrow road which wasn't the direction we should have been heading, all nine trucks had to turn round in a narrow side track, one at a time. Remember, this was the best RCT Squadron in BAOR. I was the tail end Charlie truck and therefore the last to turn round, I parked up behind Driver Harding who was parked up behind Driver Stewart and both were fighting to stay awake, they lost. Whereas I had been asleep for about four days, my two comrades in arms hadn't had more than twelve hours sleep in four days, and after waiting in line for about five minutes I got out of my cab to find out why we hadn't moved off, I found an exhausted Driver

Stewart and Driver Harding both collapsed over their steering wheels and snoring like a couple of drunken sailors. The other seven wagons had moved off and were presumably heading in the right direction. After a quick Chinese parliament we came to the same conclusion, none of us had any idea where we were supposed to be going or where we were at that moment in time. I discarded 'Stews' plan as unworkable, he thought we should wait where we were in the hope that someone would come along and find us. As they could hardly keep their eyes open and clearly weren't thinking straight, I told them to get some shut eye for a couple of hours whilst I finished the remaining chapters of 'Wheels of Terror'. The couple of hour's turned out to be an awful lot of hours and we were woken up in the morning by some soldiers of the Royal Pioneer Corps, the Section Commander from A Troop had sent out a search party to find us. We followed the 'Chunkies' Land Rover to another ammunition dump and unloaded our not very precious cargo; the Section Commander from A Troop had left instructions for us to report back to 9 Squadrons' hide which was now located in a wood on the other side of a town called Gronau.

We picked up the Tac Signs (Military Tactical Road Signs giving coded numbers directing specific troops to a given location) for 9 Squadrons Hide, after reversing into my designated bay in the wood, I had started to scrim up when 2nd Lieutenant McMahon walked past me and said, "Hello Driver Clacy, have you been having a nice time? I think Mr Bell wants to see you." Lieutenant Bell was C troop's Commander and I found him in the Squadron G1098 drinking a mug of tea, "Good grief, can this really be the elusive Driver Clacy of 9 Squadron, where the heck have you been old boy?" I told him the whole sorry tale including how 'Gus' and I got lost, the bits about us having to turn round because the Section Commander from A Troop went the wrong way, and how the two lads fell asleep and we lost contact with the convoy. I then asked the Troopie, "Sir! Will Brigadier Attack still believe we are the best RCT Squadron in BAOR"? He replied, and I quote, "Probably not Driver Clacy, but I wouldn't lose too much sleep over it".

DON'T MESS WITH THE RCT

On my second tour of duty in Northern Ireland, I was in a location near the border of Ulster and Eire in South Armagh. The army outpost was a couple of miles North East of a town called Newry, living conditions for all the soldiers was…how can I put this…cosy. The RCT room was no bigger than 14 ft by 9 ft and was home to four, three tier bunk beds, one for each of the RCT Drivers, four 6ft steel lockers (three men had to share each locker), a 3ft square dining table in the middle of the room with four tubular steel chairs around it, six .30 Browning medium machine guns and their boxes of ammunition, twelve 7.62mm Self Loading Rifles, two 9mm Browning pistols, fourteen Drivers helmets and flack jackets, a television perched on top of one of the steel lockers, oh yes, and occasionally we had an interloping huge black rat that visited us now and again. There was only one small window in the room, this was in the top right hand corner of our lodgings and it gave us some constant ventilation due to the fact that one of the panes of glass was broken. The place stank of gun oil, sweaty feet and farts, a heady aroma I think you'll agree.

I was to share this very cramped abode for the next six months with Lance Corporal Paul Paisey and Driver's Cefn (before you ask, I think it's Welsh) Bartlett, Jock Blackwood, Nev Lacey, 'Chalky' Morgan (I'm not racist, that was what everyone called him in 1977), Mark Rathbone and Frank Thomas. For the life of me, I can't remember the names of the other four Driver's, our Section Commander Corporal John Chowanski had his own private broom cupboard to sleep in, he needed it too because RCT Drivers were constantly disturbing each other due to patrol changeovers and emergency call-outs at all times of the day and night. With a dozen blokes living on top of each other in extremely cramped conditions, tensions can rise quite rapidly and often that tension ends with the odd bit of violence, some-times even the odd sneer from your best mate can invoke a right royal punch-up. Anyone who has never lived like this and might want to try the experience, may I suggest you move into your cupboard under the stairs for a couple of days with a couple of mates. It won't take long before one of you gets the right royal hump with one of the others just because of the way he breathes. And if too often someone let's rip with horrendously smelling farts, then all hell can break loose. After the fight has ended though, if you are soldiers in the British Army you just shake hands and get on with being mates again.

Space was so limited in Newry that our Saracen Armoured Personnel Carriers (RCT Driver's always referred to them as 'Cans') were parked out on the main road; this made them vulnerable to an RPG 7 (Rocket Propelled Grenade) attack or someone sneaking up at night and putting a bomb underneath them. Because of this problem a Sanger was built right next to the vehicles and was manned 24 hours a day by soldiers from the resident infantry Company. We always reversed our Cans up to the kerbstone so they faced the middle of the road ready to deploy quickly, the Cans turrets held .30 Browning machine guns in them, which were installed and removed by the RCT Driver's before and after every patrol, they were also loaded and unloaded with a box of 250 rounds of belted ammunition at the same time. Every fifth round in the ammo box was a tracer projectile that burned very brightly so the gun operator could see where his rounds were hitting even in daylight. Once loaded, the Browning's pointed straight at the front bedroom window of the house on the opposite side of the road.

One of the Squadrons from 8 Regiment RCT was based in Newry on the tour prior to ours and they followed the same procedures; but when they reversed up to the kerbstones they kept hitting the telephone pole that held the telephone wire of the house opposite. Naturally the homeowner got annoyed after his phone was disconnected on several occasions and he started complaining to the resident Infantry Company Commander in Newry. At one stage he apparently stood outside the locations' gates and became very vocal and abusive. It's not for me to speculate whether or not the 8 Regiment RCT lads were doing this out of sheer devilment, but suffice it to say, we in 17 Squadron, 10 Regiment RCT, were told it seemed to happen a lot more regularly after the bloke started to complain.

One night during the 8 Regiment RCT tour, one of their Drivers was preparing his 'Can' ready for a patrol; he put the Browning in its cradle and screwed in the two securing bolts. He then secured the box of ammo in the frame next to the gun and then lifted the top cover to load the weapon with a belt of ammunition, after closing the top cover over the ammo belt; the first parade on the gun was completed. To fire the Browning you had to pull the cocking handle on the right hand side of the gun and then squeeze the trigger on the gun cradle and the weapon will fire. I want to make it clear that we never cocked the weapon whilst first parading the gun ready for a patrol; the weapon would only be cocked just prior to opening fire. Directly opposite the parked Saracens lived the angry Irishman whose telephone wire kept getting knocked down by Drivers of the Royal Corps of

Transport. He was living in a house that was directly in front of the potential firing line of at least two loaded .30 calibre Browning machine guns, and if the gun was cocked and negligently discharged into his bedroom, well, I'm sure the Company Commander in Newry would never hear the last of it from our nit-picking Irish neighbour. So, I want to make this absolutely clear that cocking the machine gun during the first parade, well, that would plainly be a dangerous and fucking stupid thing to do.

Maybe the Driver was very tired; maybe his mind was otherwise occupied on a personal tragedy, or maybe his wife/girlfriend back in England had mentioned in her last letter that she had recently bumped into her old boyfriend at a disco, whatever the reason, the RCT Driver absent-mindedly cocked the Browning machine gun and it fired straight through the bedroom window of the house opposite. Too add to this problem some of the working parts on the Browning's were old and worn, the sear was particularly badly worn and the machine gun had a runaway when it was fired, this meant that the gun continued to fire even when pressure was taken off the trigger. The only way to stop the gun from firing was to twist the ammunition belt and even if you had the reactions of Bruce Lee, at least half a dozen rounds would be fired before you could twist the belt. Because this incident happened in Ireland it seems appropriate to use the expression 'Murphy's law', and it was 'Murphy's Law' that the Driver had a runaway with about eight rounds that smashed the bedroom window and punched a .30 calibre art nouveau design into the bedroom wall just above the house owners head. This Negligent Discharge also made the bloke in the house opposite have a shit in his pyjamas; he then dived out of bed and took cover in the bathroom. A lot of diplomacy had to be used by the British Army as the Driver headed off to the Military Corrective Training Centre in Colchester to start his 84 days incarceration.

CASUALTY LIST

During the tour in South Armagh, 17 Squadron RCT suffered four casualties of which I know about and I was one of them; Corporal John 'Scouse' Chapman and Drivers Nev Lacey and Mike Shmitz were the other three. Scouse Chapman's trauma was the least dramatic of all these but none the less painful, he quite simply discovered a way of silently closing the heavy turret hatch on a Saracen using his finger. Scouse didn't copyright his new system because he realised that the system could only be used ten times before he ran out of fingers and thumbs.

Driver Nev Lacey's injury had a bit of farce about it, he was driving the front Makrolon (very tough plastic material) short wheel based Land Rover of a two vehicle patrol, and in the usual RCT manner he was driving it faster than was strictly permitted. He and his three accompanying infantrymen were travelling downhill on a rough track just off the main Dublin to Belfast road. As he approached a left hand bend he realised he was going too fast and the vehicle tipped over onto its right hand side. Nev broke his right arm in the accident and although the infantry were a bit shaken up, they didn't suffer any injuries. The vehicle had tipped over a slight ridge and was lying on its right side with the roof of the vehicle facing down a steep one in three hill. Like all military vehicles, the Makrolon Land Rover was a tough little son of a bitch and was drivable even after Nev had tipped it over on its side, but the eight soldiers on the mobile patrol would have to get it back on its wheels first. The six infantrymen and other RCT Driver tried to push the Land Rover back up onto its wheels, but because of the steep incline and the force of gravity, it made the job impossible.

The infantry Section Commander came up with a foolproof plan, "Let's roll the Rover downhill onto it's roof, we can then roll it over again so it is lying on it's left side, then all we have to do is roll it over one more time and lift it back onto it's wheels. The Land Rover had four wheel drive with a high/low ratio gearbox so it should have been easy to drive it back up the hill. The Green Jacket patrol Commander said, "It will save us the embarrassment of having to radio for a REME recovery truck to pull us out of the shit." It was a plan doomed to failure, you the reader already know what was about to happen even before I started writing this story, the lads started the first phase of the plan but then the steep incline and the force of gravity got together with the laws of physics. All eight soldiers stood around and watched as their stricken vehicle rolled over and over down the hill, it was lucky that the hedge at the bottom stopped it going any further. The patrol had the embarrassing task of requesting a REME recovery vehicle to pull the completely wrecked Land Rover 70 meters back up the hill. The Land Rover wasn't drivable after recovery.

The injury Mike Shmitz suffered was a lot more serious and was the result of an attack by the IRA on the small outpost at Forkhill, which was located very close to the border with Southern Ireland. The terrorists who carried out any attacks on the Forkhill location could do so with impunity, once they had discharged their weapons they just had to dash a short distance to safety over the border and into Eire. Soldiers of the British Army could neither fire their weapons over the border nor pursue the gunmen to apprehend them. Forkhill was used as a base from which the army could send out foot patrols, but all the IRA had to do was watch and wait for the area to be clear of patrols and then hotfoot it just over the border to make their attack. As far as the IRA was concerned the attack would then be legitimately carried out in Northern Ireland and the Eire Government could not be called to account for an attack from within their border. The constant need for foot-patrols meant the 'Cans' in Forkhill were rarely used and so the two RCT Drivers, Lance Corporal Andy Keeler and Driver Mike Shmitz, constantly volunteered to go out on 'Footsies' with the resident infantry Company.

On the day that Mike Shmitz was injured he was resting on his bed, the IRA mortared the location and scored a hit very close to the RCT accommodation. Mike sustained shrapnel wounds to his feet and he had to be flown to Musgrave Park military wing at the Royal Victoria Hospital in Belfast for surgery. From what I remember he didn't return to duty during the rest of the tour in South Armagh. He was replaced at Forkhill by my old mate Driver Johnny Walker.

As for me, well, I was knocked unconscious by a car that was driving though the mobile Vehicle Checkpoint in which I was working on the Dublin Road, my right ear was badly lacerated and I was evacuated by a Saracen ambulance to the army Medical Centre in Bessbrook. The Royal Army Medical Corps doctor on duty that night sutured my ear back into roughly the same shape it was prior to the accident. I then returned to Newry and after packing up my personal kit, I was taken to B Troop headquarters in Ballykinler to recuperate for a couple of weeks. We four were lucky, although the head injury I sustained resulted in me getting type 1 diabetes; at least I got to go home and continue with my life, as did John, Nev and Mick. For others it was a much more horrific and sadder story.

The Royal Corps of Transport has operated and supported every unit that has ever deployed on Operation Banner from 1970 onwards. In that time we as a Corps have lost nineteen of our comrades. If you compare that to the Royal Ulster Constabulary and other regiments that have also served in the province, the number is quite low, but none the less these RCT soldiers have all paid the ultimate price so that others can live in peace.

Major P Cowley, 13/01/70, Died on Duty.
Corporal C Young, 29/07/71, RTA.
Driver S Beedie, 26/03/72, RTA.
Driver L Jubb, 26/04/72, RTA after mob attack.
LCpl M Bruce, 31/05/72, IRA sniper.
SSgt J Fleming, 09/07/72, IRA sniper.
Driver P Heppenstall, 14/07/72, IRA sniper.
Driver S Cooper, 21/07/72, IRA car bomb.
Driver R Kitchen, 10/11/72, IRA sniper.
Driver M Gay, 17/03/73, IRA landmine.
Sergeant T Penrose, 24/03/73, Murdered whilst off-duty.
Corporal A Gilmour, 29/08/73, RTA.
LCpl E Crosbie, 23/11/73, RTA.
Driver N McKenzie, 11/04/74, IRA landmine.
Driver H J King, 19/04/75, RTA.
Driver W Knight, 17/05/76, RTA.
Driver V Dormer, 01/10/76, Cause of death unknown.
Sergeant W Edgar, 15/04/77, Abducted and murdered.
Lieutenant N Brewer, 31/05/79, Cause of death unknown.
Driver J Dorrity, 30/09/79, Cause of death unknown.
Driver S Atkins, 29/11/80, RTA.
Driver I MacDonald, 08/03/81, Cause of death unknown.
Driver P Bulman, 19/05/81, IRA landmine.

Driver P Johns, 25/10/81, Cause of death unknown.
Captain J Meadows, 08/08/84, Cause of death unknown.
LCpl N Duncan, 22/02/89, Shot by IRA.
Driver T Gibson,n20/10/89, Murdered by IRA.
Driver C Pantry, 02/11/91, Killed by IRA bomb.

We must remember them.

BALLYKINLER BEACH

Cefn Bartlett was sent a bottle of Asbach Brandy in the post by his German girlfriends' father; he sent it out to our location in Newry so Cefn could celebrate his nineteenth birthday. Standard Operating Procedures whilst on Operational tours in Ulster decreed that, "Whilst serving in Northern Ireland all Military Personnel are restricted to the maximum consumption of no more than two cans of beer in a 24 hour period. Anyone consuming alcohol must not be on essential duties. Under no circumstances must hard spirits like whiskey or brandy be consumed at any time. Anyone contravening these orders will be subject to the full weight of Military Law." I have to point out that there wasn't a sub-clause in these orders that stated, "Oh, by the way, in the event of an RCT Driver having a birthday during their tour, they have our permission to get completely trolleyed." This is in fact what Driver Cefn Bartlett did. He very generously shared the bottle with all his RCT mates but unfortunately quaffed a bit too much of it himself, I can remember Cefn lying face down on the top of one of the 6ft steel lockers (Don't ask me what he was doing up there) and singing an Irish Rebel song. It all got a bit too much for Cefn and he proceeded to projectile vomit down the side of the locker and over two of our .30 Browning machine guns.

Although we RCT Drivers found the whole incident very funny, the Location Duty Sergeant who walked into our room to investigate the appalling singing didn't. The smell of brandy-laced sick did not improve the rooms' fragrance of gun oil, sweaty feet and farts. Cefn was lucky a decent Sergeant had caught him in that state, the 2 RGJ (Royal Green Jackets) NCO could have thrown the book at him and he would definitely have ended up doing time in the nick. The Sergeant gave Cefn the bollocking of a life time and made him clean up the two machine guns (he did this whilst continuing to vomit into a bucket), he also told Cefn to report to the cook Sergeant in the morning because as punishment, he was going to have to clean an awful lot of pots and pans for the Army Catering Corps.

This wasn't the only incident when Cefn got into trouble, the second time he ended up being put on a charge by a different Duty Sergeant, Cefn even today, over thirty years later, states that the incident was a joke that went wrong, and yet he ended up in the clink for 14 days. One night whilst on Sanger duty in the High tower at Newry, Cefn was keeping his eyes peeled through the three sliding metal hatches when he heard a knock on the bolted door behind him. It was Driver Frank Thomas, "Cefn, there's an incoming phone call for you on the payphone in the location foyer; apparently it is your girlfriend in Germany." Cefn unbolted the door and told Frank, "If I leave this post during my stag I'll get into a whole world of shit. Can you ask her to phone me back in about an hour?" Frank rather generously offered to stag on for Cefn whilst he took the phone call. As he was heading towards the payphone Cefn was collared by the Duty Sergeant who had posted him in the Sanger just over an hour previously, "What the fuck are you doing Driver Bartlett, you should be on watch in the main tower, explain yourself." "I'm just taking a phone call from my girlfriend; someone is covering for me in the Sanger." The suspicious Green Jacket Sergeant was having none of it and he frog marched Cefn back to the Sanger only to find it was empty, Frank wasn't there. Had Cefn got to the phone he would have found the receiver off the hook but no-one on the end of the line, it was Frank's idea of a joke. He assumed Cefn would realise he had been the butt of a lame joke and then would've headed straight back to the Sanger to complete his stag on sentry; Frank hadn't envisaged Cefn bumping into the Duty Sergeant. Major D Gibley RCT was the Officer Commanding of 17 Squadron RCT and he came down to Newry from Long Kesh to preside over Cefn's military charge. Cefn didn't squeal on Frank and offered no defence against the charge. On the evidence presented to the OC he had no option but to find Driver Bartlett RCT guilty as charged and awarded him 14 days in the nick at Ballykinler.

It was shortly after Cefn started his two-week break in the Black Watch Holiday Camp that I sustained my head injury and I also headed off to Ballykinler to recuperate, Driver Steve Tong replaced me at the Newry Location. Accommodation at the massive Ballykinler camp was very good because all the buildings were similar to a brick built camp in the UK. Each of the large bright and airy rooms was home to about ten soldiers and not a bunk bed was to be found anywhere. At first it was strange not to be woken up at all hours with someone jostling on one of the two bunks underneath me; it was wonderful to have a living space bigger than a rabbit hutch. I reported to B Troop office where I found Second Lieutenant Strachan the Troop Commander, Staff Sergeant 'Mac' McKinley the MT Staff Sergeant, and Sergeant Pearn our Admin Sergeant. They asked what happened when I was knocked down in the VCP and then briefed me on what I would be doing for the next couple of weeks. The spare Saracens in B Troops' hanger had to be driven for a minimum of 10 miles every day to make sure they remained in good working order; just in case they were needed at any one of B Troops' Locations to replace a damaged or unserviceable vehicle. On the south side of the camp was an amazing sandy beach that was about eight miles long, and when the tide went out the beach was over a mile deep. My job for the next fortnight was simply to drive these spare 'Cans' up and down the beach until they had clocked up the necessary mileage. Every time any of these APC's went out of the back gate and onto the beach, the driver had to have a commander in the turret because the vision from the driving position in a Saracen was notoriously poor.

In 1977/78 the army had to adapt the Alvis Saracen because they were constantly overheating whilst out on patrols, we were now using the FF Alvis Saracen, which had a cowling on the front to force fresh cold air though the engine compartment. The cowling was made out of a thin metal that was curved over the front of the radiator grill and was held semi-rigid by some tough rubber material at the sides. This cured the overheating problem.

After settling into the Ballykinler way of life the little jaunts up and down the beach became boring, particularly if only one Saracen was out there at a time, it was much more fun to chase each other up and down the sand dunes and onto the beach with about four 'Cans' out there. One day my old mate Johnny Walker and I were the only Drivers available to take the Saracens out on their daily exercise, when I asked him if he wanted to drive or command he said, "Fuck that Harry! Let's take one each, you won't need a commander because we will be the only vehicles out there, and anyway there's over 8 miles of beach, we couldn't possibly hit each other." Rather stupidly I replied, "Oh yeah! That's a good idea." The Black Watch sentry opened the back gate and let

Johnny and I roar past him, Johnny led the way and headed straight past the dunes and towards the sea. Because the sand was so flat and firm Johnny screamed his Saracen up through the five gears until he reached the 'Cans' top speed of 50 mph. I did the same in my vehicle and stayed quite close to the back of Johnny, he wasn't about to let me overtake him, in the world of RCT Drivers' you are a complete tosser if someone overtakes you whilst you're at full throttle. As he approached the sea I could see Johnny was starting to make a wide left hand turn and he drove out into the sea and drove parallel with the shoreline. He was so far out that the bottom third of his wheels were under water, I rather stupidly followed him but kept slightly behind and to the left of his 'Can'. The seawater from his wheels came flying into my driving compartment and not only saturated me, the mixture of salt water and sand diminished my vision. I steered to the left to get into shallower water and away from the spray Johnny's vehicle was throwing into my Can; unfortunately Johnny did exactly the same but cut a more acute curve. I caught the back wing of Johnny's APC with my front cowling and the loud bang instantly told me this was not going to go down well with Staff Sergeant 'Mac' MacKinley. Johnny stopped his Saracen and climbed out of the front hatch; he then walked down the vehicles left hand catwalk and jumped down onto the beach. As I was climbing out of the front hatch Johnny started laughing at my drenched combat jacket and shouted, "Clacy! You fucking wanker!" The cowling on my Saracen was badly dented on the right side and Johnny's rear left hand light cluster was a total mess, and yet Johnny seemed totally unconcerned, "Come on Harry, lets get these two heaps of shit back to the hanger."

The Black Watch sentry on the back gate also laughed when he saw my damaged cowling and he waved at me with a clenched fist. Once parked up in the hanger Johnny went to the tool store and came back with a 4lb lump hammer and a tin of olive green paint. With all the finesse of a rhinoceros Johnny set about straightening my damaged cowling and his light cluster, after slapping a load of olive green paint on the scratched paintwork and replacing the rear bulbs and ruby's, Johnny stood back and admired his handiwork. "Job done and it's as good as new mate, it also saves having to write out a shit load of paperwork."

BLACK SARACEN AWARDS

During 17 Squadrons tour of South Armagh, our Headquarters produced the same sort of Squadron monthly journal that was distributed when we were based back in BAOR, a completely black silhouetted side view of a Saracen APC was on the front of every recurrent periodical. There were jokes, notifications of births within the squadron, postings in and out; and it also included articles that the wives back in West Germany had submitted so that married soldiers of the squadron felt a closer contact with home. Furthermore each publication also had a selection of photographs that were taken of soldiers from the Squadron at work in the Province and those competing in football, rugby and boxing competitions. One publication included pictures of our 10 Regiment RCT Pin-up (Sandy Macateer), both she and our Commanding Officer, Lieutenant Colonel Skipper RCT, came to visit the scattered locations in which we were deployed. Sandy was a real morale booster; mainly because in the previous two months most of us hadn't got up close and personal with an attractive and beautifully scented woman, well, not one who wasn't spitting at us and shouting, "Fuck off back to England you British Bastard". Sandy Macateer did a great job of smiling and chatting whilst sitting on an Officers or Drivers lap, she probably thought it was a Northern Ireland Baton Round sticking in her back during the many photo sessions.

Someone within 17 Squadron RCT came up with the idea of bestowing joke awards to Drivers, NCO's and Officers in the Squadron, because of the silhouetted profile of the Saracen on the front of the Squadrons' monthly magazine, the honours were called 'The Black Saracen Awards'.

These less than prestigious accolades were bestowed on any individual deemed to have made a cluster-fuck in a particular field of their own idiocy; they were varied and were meant to make fun of the clown who had made a particular blunder. Nominations were sent in for the final squadron publication before leaving Ireland, and soldiers being soldiers, a lot of the suggestions were unprintable; however, the Chief Clerk managed to assemble enough (ones that didn't refer to certain parts of a soldiers' anatomy) to fill his deadline before publication went ahead.

The winners of the 1977 Black Saracen Awards were awarded to the following nominee's:

1. **For Devotion**. For his dedication above and beyond the call of duty, this award went to Driver Webb who forgot to go on his four days Rest and Recuperation leave.
2. **For Literary Extravaganza**. This award was given to Sergeant Scott's wife who had sent 137 letters to her husband during the tour. She must have written a letter every day.
3. **For Finance**. This one went to the Army Pay Office in Bielefeld who sent the Married Quarters Fuel and Light Rebates out to the husbands serving in Northern Ireland. God bless the incompetent clerks of the Royal Army Pay Corps. Unlucky girls.
4. **For Stating The Bleedin' Obvious**. When Driver Allman was asked by a REME mechanic which headlight on his 'Pig' needed replacing, he raised his eyebrows and said, "The broken one you idiot."
5. **Zulu Warrior Dancer of the Tour**. After considering the many nominations throughout the

Squadron, it was presented to Driver Abraham. He won this award for his style and allure as his combat trousers fell to his rather plump ankles.

6. **Holiday Centre of the Year**. This award went to the Black Watch Guardroom in Ballykinler. Only five Drivers from the Squadron voted against this, the most vocal was Driver Cefn Bartlett.

7. **For Constantly Making the Most Irritating Noise**. There was a dead heat on the final count for this award so it was finally shared between the Army Dog Unit Kennels and Driver Heath.

8. **For contributing the most money to offset the high cost of our Squadrons' Deployment to South Armagh**. The Ministry of Defence heartily thanked Driver Walker for the sum of money he donated through his Officer Commanding, after marching into the OC's office for an interview without coffee he explained, "Sir, I only realised I had lost my MOD 90 (Military Identity Card) after someone else had found it."

9. **For inventivness**. This was a shared prize between Driver Ustinowski and Corporal 'Scouse' Chapman, they both introduced and personally tested a new silent method of slamming down Saracen hatches using their fingers.

10. **Survivors of the Tour who can still smile at Breakfast**. To all in 9 Squadron (Main) RCT in Moscow Camp, for spending four months with you know who! (9 Squadron RCT were supporting units in the Belfast area while 17 Squadron were in South Armagh. For those who can't remember who the dig was aimed at, it was their OC Major 'Freddie' Crabbe RCT. Trust me, on any day of the week you

would rather have had the other type of crab irritating you.)

WHAT WOULD YOUR MOTHER THINK?

After getting injured in South Armagh (see 'Harry was a Crap Hat' page 85), I returned to Bielefeld with the rest of the Squadron after completing the tour. Within months of 17 Squadrons return from South Armagh I started to lose weight and was incredibly tired and thirsty at all times of the day and night. I could have won a national pissing competition with the amount of uric acid that was passing through my bladder and kidneys. At the Medical Centre in Bielefeld I was eventually diagnosed as having Type 1 diabetes and so RCT Manning and Records posted me back to 66 Squadron RCT who were based in Tidworth, this posting was instigated to get me and my family back to the UK so I could be medically discharged from the army. The process of getting me out of the army became a bit like a Brian Rix farce, but more about that later in Ex Dentibus Ensis. Prior to the RAMC trying to discharge me from the army I became 66 Squadron RCT's' Regimental Medical Assistant for a couple of years.

During my time as a Regimental Medical Assistant, 66 Squadron RCT took part in a massive NATO Military Exercise in Denmark called 'Exercise Amber Express', and I went along as the Squadron medic which was my sole job for the six weeks we were away from Tidworth Garrison. Anyone who had any medical maladies reported it to the Squadron Sergeant Major first thing in the morning and then reported to me for the appropriate diagnosis and treatment. I had been a Regimental Medical Assistant for well over a year and whilst back in Tidworth I worked day to day in the Garrison Medical Centre doing pretty much the same thing I was now going to do out in the field. I could suture wounds, give First Aid treatment for just about any medical emergency and whilst on the Exercise I could even prescribe a certain amount of drugs that I carried in my medical treatment box. You wouldn't believe the kit medics used to carry about on Exercise in our Field Medical Kits, antibiotics, intravenous fluids, giving sets and cannulas, morphine, scalpels, forceps, it was like a miniature hospital inside a three foot by two foot metal suitcase with a red cross on it.

Our Squadron was located in a field just outside the city of Holbaek and on one particular afternoon I was skiving on my camp bed reading a Sven Hassel book when my friend Corporal Paul Paisey came in to have a chat. "Harry, one of our young Drivers' went into Copenhagen yesterday and had sex with a prostitute, he doesn't know we saw him go off with her and he has surreptitiously started asking me about the signs and symptoms of venereal disease. Do you fancy doing a bit of a wind up on him?" I was slightly miffed at Paul and told him so, "For Gods sake Paul, you should know by now that you don't need to ask me if I want to be involved in a wind up, where is the young lamb and is he ready for the slaughter?" The SSM (Squadron Sergeant Major) was also in on the joke and had arranged for me to give a lecture to the whole Squadron in the cookhouse tent that night; I had to talk about venereal diseases and how to protect against them. Paul also mentioned that the prostitute the young lad had been spotted walking off with had peroxide blonde hair, and he asked if that would be of any use in the wind up. It was, and my cruel and cunning mind started working overtime on what I was going to do to the unsuspecting tethered goat.

At 2000 hours the whole Squadron were gathered in the large marquee ready for my lecture and the sandy haired young soldier, for whom this unbeknownst meeting was in aid of, was sitting on a bench seat at the front of the audience. The lecture went really well and the Squadron enjoyed both of my demonstrations of a soldier scratching his nether regions because of an infestation of pubic lice, and the painful look on my face to imitate someone trying to urinate whilst suffering from a syphilitic infection. I tried to give my students a bit of everything, entertainment as well as education. On closing the lecture I passed on the following information to my enthralled audience, "If anyone from the Squadron does take the opportunity of putting some money into the Danish economy, via a local…lady, then make sure you wear a Johnny and check her green card medical inspections are up to date. 22 Field Hospital, which is co-located with us on this Exercise, have issued all units with the following warning. Apparently a blonde haired prostitute is entertaining clients in Copenhagen and she has missed her last two medical check ups, not only is this against the law in Denmark, but you may be at risk of a pubic lice infection if you use her services". The bait had been placed and the trap was set, all I had to do now was play the waiting game. Soldiers are quick witted and astute but if you subliminally put a notion in their head; they will believe anything you tell them. As I asked if there were any questions I could see the sandy haired young soldier at the front was looking red faced and had already started to scratch his groin, the bait had been taken and the fun was about to start.

After the Squadron dispersed back to their tents the young lad hung back as I cleared my lecture stuff away, he whispered, "Harry? Could I have a quick word with you mate...I think I might have had sex with that lady you were talking about, what the fuck do I do now." I put on my serious and concerned Doctor Kildare face and asked, "Did you put on a condom before having sex with her?" He confirmed he had and I then rather dramatically said, "Phew, thank heavens for that, the only thing we have to deal with now is that you might have caught crabs, but don't worry that is easily treated." He seemed somewhat relieved with my diagnosis and prognosis. I took a large green plastic medical razor out of my treatment box and handed it over to him, these razors were used to shave a patients' hair prior to suturing a head wound. They were very similar to the old heavy and cumbersome Wilkinson Sword razors; they were very sharp but if you tried to shave with it you would, without fail, end up with cuts and a rather nasty shaving rash. "You are going to have to shave your pubic area and remove any hair that the lice will more than likely have infested." He looked unhappy with my treatment plan and asked if there was a cream or medical shampoo that would negate the need to shave his groin and testicles. I gave him the bad news that no such treatment had yet been invented and shaving was the only way to get rid of them. I had a delousing shampoo in my medical kit that he could have used, but where would the fun be in that?

We knew he had carried out the treatment because of the screams as he dabbed his private parts with surgical spirit, I gave him this to dab on his groin and testicles after he had shaved. Oh how we laughed in the Squadron as the tale was passed on from soldier to soldier; the anecdote doesn't quite end there though. Later on I was sitting on a canvas chair in my tent and checking the contents of my medical box, I heard someone behind me enter the tent and although I didn't look round I had a sixth sense someone was standing very close to me. The sandy haired soldier was standing at my left shoulder with his combat trousers and underpants round his ankles, he was holding his wedding tackle in his hand and he waved it no less than six inches from my face saying, "Does this look alright Harry!"

I THINK HE'S DEAD

After my Squadron returned to Tidworth from Denmark, I went back to my usual duties in the Garrison Medical Centre and this included doing the preliminary medical checks on soldiers prior to sending them into the doctor for various medical appointments. We had to check the patients' blood pressure, give them eye and hearing tests, and we also had to record the soldiers' temperature, pulse, and rate of respiration on the relevant treatment card. After we had done our bit, we told the soldier to sit outside the doctors' surgery and wait to be called in; we then placed the soldiers' medical file on the doctors' desk and told the quack that his next patient was waiting outside.

I use the word quack, not under advisement, but from my experience of working with some retired RAMC (Royal Army Medical Corps) doctors. Colonel (Retired) Langford was one in particular who worked as a locum in Tidworth Medical Centre; not only was he very old but he was a doddery and cantankerous old git who often had extended liquid lunches at the bar in the Officers Mess. He had a large red, and very heavily veined nose (sometimes referred to as a whiskey drinkers' nose) and he looked like an older and more haggard version of W C Grace. One of the problems, when giving a patient to a particular doctor, was that each quack had his or her own idiosyncrasies, some required every patient to have boots and socks removed ready for them to inspect their feet regardless of the reason for the appointment, and others maybe wanted them to sit stripped to the waist outside their surgery so the doctor didn't have to wait for the soldier to undress. Medics were never sure which doctor had which particular eccentric peculiarity.

After doing the usual tests on a Sapper from 22 Engineer Regiment I took him straight into Colonel Langford's surgery so he could assess the soldier, the Colonel seemed a bit confused. He spluttered and slurred, "What am I supposed to be doing with this one Corporal Clacy!" I shouted at the deaf old sod, "He's come in for a 'Fit for Diving' medical Colonel." I then went back to the main office and sat at the main reception hatch. Ten minutes later I looked up and saw the same Sapper walking towards me stripped to the waist and not wearing his socks and boots, he got a few curious glances from some of the army wives and children sitting in the main waiting room. He put his head through the hatch and quietly said, "I think he's dead." Somewhat confused and alarmed I asked, "Who's dead?" The Sapper looked over his shoulder at the surgery he had come out of and said, "The old fart that was doing my medical, I was sitting on the chair by his desk and he was listening to my heart when he just suddenly died." Several thoughts immediately ran through my mind, one, the pair of them are having a laugh at my expense, but as Colonel Langford had no sense of humour at all I immediately discarded this notion, two, Colonel Langford has had a stroke and has actually died on us, or three, well actually I rarely manage to have more than two thoughts in one day, so it was only the two thoughts that ran through my mind. And the most likely one was that the Colonel had had a stroke and croaked.

I told the young Sapper to follow me as we quickly headed back into Colonel Langford's surgery, the Colonel was sitting in the chair at his desk and was leaning forwards on his right elbow, he was also holding the business end of a stethoscope in his right hand and had the listening ends in both ears. He was sitting upright and holding the stethoscope like a safe cracker from a Carry on film but he didn't make any movement or noise as I approached the desk, I thought, 'Shit, the old boys pegged it at long last'. I started to think how sad it was that this fairly high ranking ex military doctor had ended his days still working for the British Army that he had served for so many years. The silence and eeriness in the room was palpable, I nervously felt for a radial pulse in his wrist and although his skin was warm I couldn't feel anything, I was holding an old dead gits' wrist in my hand. It was a horrible feeling. I turned to the Sapper who was standing at my shoulder and was about to ask him to go and fetch the Practice Manager when the Colonel jumped up out of his chair and shouted in my ear, "Where did he go!" The drunken old bastard had just fallen into an alcoholic based sleep and woke up when I tried to take his pulse, when he jumped up and shouted I came as close as I ever have to having a lumpy cough in my trousers.

LIEUTENANT COLONEL BELL RAMC

In the early 1980's Tidworth Garrison held a Point to Point competition that was open to all branches of the army, for anyone who hasn't served in the British Army I must explain, the majority of competitors in these 'Up their own arses' events, are from the 'Horsey Set' of the British Army's' Cavalry Regiments. The whole garrison area was invaded by Hooray Henry's and chinless wonders going by the names of Simon, Wupert and Wodney, even Pwincess Anne and her husband Captain Mark Phiwips came down from on high to take part. Even though he was married to Princess Anne, Captain Mark Phillips was still a serving officer in the Queens Dragoon Guards.

Lieutenant Colonel Bell RAMC (Royal Army Medical Corps) was an Irishman and one of the doctors at Tidworth Garrison Medical Centre, both he and I were tasked to provide medical cover for this event, we had a 12x12 tent with stretchers, trestles, and an abundance of medical equipment. We also had a large white Bedford Ambulance that could easily be painted blue and used by Pickford Removals once the army had finished with it. It was a beautiful sunny day and as no one seemed to need our medical expertise the Colonel and I sunned ourselves on a couple of army canvas chairs outside our tented Medical Centre. As we drank tea from our large black army mugs and put the world to rights, the afor mentioned Princesses' husband rode up to our little world; after pulling up his horse he looked down from his magnificent stallion and addressed the Senior Medical Officer, "Are you the Medico chappie?" The 'Doc' looked at me and then back up at 'His Royal Highness' Captain Mark Phillips; he said in his lilting

Southern Irish accent, "Are you talking to me Captain, because if you are, I expect you to get off that shitting machine and address me in the manner more becoming of your senior officer. Do you understand me Captain?" For the first time in my life I had an affiliation with a member of the Royal family, Captain Mark Phillips and I were both gob smacked. But there our similarities ended, because HRH wasn't used to being talked to in that manner and he rode off with the huff; whereas, I was used to being talked to like that and I nearly pissed myself laughing whilst not riding a horse.

A couple of minutes later, Captain Mark Phillips equerry (it's always mystified me that when a junior officer marries into the HRH world, they get a more senior officer as a flunky), the flunky was a Major and also a Cavalry Officer, he came riding up to our little world. He also pulled up his horse in front of the Colonel and looked down on the 'Doc' before saying in his ten bob accent, "The Officer you have just addressed is Princess Anne's husband and he is furious, how dare you talk to a member of the Royal Family in that manner"! The 'Doc' jumped to his feet and shouted, "And how fucking dare you as a Major, talk to a Lieutenant Colonel In the Royal Army Medical Corps in such a demeaning manner, I am yours, and his, superior Officer, now get off that fucking old nag, put your heels together, and speak to me in a more appropriate manner"! An irate Irishman in full flight is an awesome spectacle.

The Major didn't get off his old nag; instead he yanked on the reins of his horse and galloped away to the safety of his HRH mate. The 'Doc' came back to his canvas chair, sat down and said, "Now, what were we talking about before we were so rudely interrupted".

EX DENTIBUS ENSIS

'Ex Dentibus Ensis' is the motto of the Royal Army Dental Corps and it is incorporated on the base of their soldier's cap badges, it is a Latin quotation that means, "From the teeth comes the sword". The cap badge also has the head of a dragon with a sword in its mouth and the whole badge is surrounded by a laurel wreath. Greek mythology has an awful lot to answer for; my favourite of all the different myths is the one that comes from the Greek fable of 'Jason and the Argonauts'. Jason and his plucky bunch of trailblazers set off on a quest to find a golden fleece and along the way they get involved in quite a few punch-ups. In one of these scuffles their nemeses use the teeth from the jaw of a dead dragon to resurrect some skeletons, these armed dead carcasses then attack our heroes who fight them off and eventually escape. I think the British Army saw a parallel of this story that was suitable for the Royal Army Dental Corps; if the Corps maintained the British Army's dental health then it was indirectly providing the means to fight a war. Yawn! Any soldier who is suffering from toothache is not going to be a motivated and efficient fighting warrior. Yawn again!

In the First World War when Field Marshall Haig suffered from toothache he was attended by an RAMC doctor who said, "I'm sorry sir, but we don't have any dentists serving within the ranks of the British Army. I will arrange for a top French civilian dentist to come and administer to your needs here in your opulent chateau, would you like me to help you back to bed so you are more comfortable whilst I wipe your arse for you"? Maybe this is the reason why the British Army suffered 60,000 casualties on the first day of the

Battle of the Somme in 1916; the probability is that Haig totally buggered up sixty thousand soldiers, and their families lives, purely because he couldn't understand the intricacies of using a toothbrush. Officers? I ask you. A Corps had yet to be established to deal with the routine dental problems in the British Army, at the start of the Great War all serious maxillofacial injuries were dealt with by RAMC surgeons and civilian dental surgeons who had been recruited into the Army Medical Services. It was pretty much the same for a Tommy in the trenches, and as an 'Other Rank' he would have been dealt with in pretty much the same manner as old 'Haigie' by the same sort of doctor, "Private Smith! You are a malingering pest, if you report sick with toothache again I will have you shot for wasting my time. Now fuck off out of my sight you obnoxious little shit".

Meanwhile, back to my own particular problems, the Army Medical Services were trying to coerce me into leaving the army because I was now an insulin dependent diabetic. The Royal Corps of Transport needed soldiers who were both physically and medically fit, by law I couldn't even drive an HGV Class 3 wagon and that was the minimum requirement to be in the RCT. I refused to leave though and argued black was blue with the Royal Army Medical Corps doctors sitting on my medical board, I wanted to stay in the British Army because I had signed on the dotted line for a contract of 9/22 years, and if they wanted me out they would have to literally rip the uniform off my body and physically throw me out of the camp gates. I did tell them that if they chose to adopt that technique of getting rid of me, I would simply climb back over the wall and make a real nuisance of myself. I was also a married man with three young children (the eldest two, Matt and Naomi came from Ronnie's first marriage and Daniel came from our marriage), these three children needed feeding and clothing and were dependant on me to provide them with a decent standard of living; as a Type 1 diabetic my future career options out of the army were limited. I didn't want to leave the army and end up knocking on the Local Councils' door begging for a council house and trying to scrounge some money from the social services.

Because I stubbornly refused to leave the British Army and the RAMC Medical Board stubbornly refused to see things my way, it appeared we were at an impasse. One of the doctors on the board came up with an idea, "Lance Corporal Clacy! If you can find a Corps or Regiment that will allow you to transfer into their ranks and still gain promotion at your medical grading, then this board will allow you to stay in the army; if you can't find another trade at your grading then you will have to agree to leave." I accepted the challenge and put in a hefty amount of transfer requests to just about every branch of the army, I was granted two career interviews, the first invitation was with the RAMC (this was the Corps that was trying to throw me out of the army) and I was interviewed by a Full Colonel in Medical Headquarters South Eastern District. He thanked me for my interest in transferring into his Corps but as I was currently under a review from a Medical Board he couldn't actually agree to my transfer into the RAMC. "Let us see what happens on your next appointment with the Medical Board, if they agree to your transfer to another Corps then I will be more than glad to accept you into the RAMC in a third line role". The frustration was starting to get to me, "But the Medical Board have said that if I can get a transfer into any branch of the army, they will let me stay, so if you agree to a transfer then they will have to let me stay in the army, sir". He wouldn't be pressurised into making a decision, "If I allow you to transfer into the RAMC and my medical colleagues are recalcitrant about you staying; then surely the Royal Army Medical Corps would look hypocritical, indecisive and incompetent. No, before I can make a decision about you Lance Corporal Clacy, I think I will have to wait for the result of your Medical Board. Please close the door on your way out". Here endeth the lesson on me transferring into the RAMC.

It was lucky for me that the Commanding Officer of No 3 Dental Group in Tidworth wasn't as indecisive as the doctors of the RAMC, Colonel Brocklebank L/RADC interviewed me and said, "There will always be a vacancy within the ranks of the Royal Army Dental Corps for a smart and keen Junior NCO like you Lance Corporal Clacy". I went back to the Medical Board and told them of my good news, to be fair all three of the 'old farts' congratulated me on my fortitude on finding another career in the army. We all parted on good terms and I transferred into the RADC within a couple of months after being put on the next available Dental Clerical Assistants course. The RADC was made up of approximately 20% soldiers who were TFI's (Transfer in's) from other Corps and Regiments of the British Army, the RADC direct entrant 'soldiers' (pardon my mirth from using the word soldier in this context) made up about another 40-50%, and last but by no means least, the rest of the Corps was made up of QARANC's (Queen Alexandra Royal Army Nursing Corps, or Quick And Ready And Never Caught). The QARANC's all wore their Corps regulation grey uniforms and Cap Badges, but they did wear a small RADC broach on the lapel of their jumpers and service dress, this designated them as being attached to the RADC. Note: - On the 1st April 1992 all QARANC's who worked in the Army Dental Services were involuntarily transferred to the RADC and had to start wearing RADC cap badges, uniforms, headdress and staple belts, it was a sad day for all the female Dental Clerical Assistant's and Dental Hygienist's, one ex QA has pointed out to me that they joined the fuckwits of the RADC on 'April fool's day'. QARANC's! Don't you just love them?

In 'Harry was a Crap Hat' I give the RADC a bit of a hard time, not just about the Corps' role within the army; but I've also written about some of the pathetic and vindictively gutless toadies who hid behind their sycophantically earned rank, trust me, I'm no longer bitter about them. Every one of these crawlers was a direct entrant into the RADC; none of them had done any hard time soldiering in one of the British Army's stouter Corps or Regiments. I also wrote about some of the great guys I also met within the Corps (some were direct entrants) and I'm going to do the same in this chapter of the book, the RADC is usually sneered at by other Corps and Regiments in the British Army, let's face it, as far as they were concerned we were all just a bunch of effeminate dental nurses, hardly a very macho career for a soldier of the British Army. As I've already admitted, I've given the Royal Army Dental Corps a bit of a verbal and written bashing, but in all honesty I think I owe the Corps a debt of gratitude. If they hadn't taken me in I wouldn't now be receiving a full army pension and I also wouldn't have made some of the best friends any man could wish to have chanced upon. I wrote in 'Harry was a Crap Hat' about my friends Corporal Jeff Bush, Lance Corporal Paul Harrat and Private 'Pip' Green who transferred into the Corps with me, and I also wrote at length about the indomitable Sergeant's 'Ritchie' John and John King who remain friends to this very day, you can call in and see them after a decades absence and continue with a conversation that you finished ten years earlier. Both of these men haven't changed one iota since leaving the army, maybe a little less hair on the head and a bit more in the ears and nose, but they're both still very fit men who have retained their unique military sense of humour. I want to set the record straight though that not all soldiers in the RADC are a bunch of spineless wimps, some of them were extremely tough men. Here are two hard men who also transferred into the Corps, two men whom I hold in the very highest of esteem and if the shit ever hit the fan, these are two men like Ritchie and John King who you'd definitely want standing beside you.

Sergeant Steve Roberts RADC

I met Sergeant Steve Roberts at Headquarters No 4 Dental Group in Camberley during a Military Training day, once a year all RADC soldiers had to run a 3 mile BFT (Basic Fitness Test), fire a personal weapon on the ranges and do some practical tests on First Aid and NBC (Nuclear Biological and Chemical Warfare). It was like dipping your toe in to test the temperature of the water; the RADC very rarely dived in headfirst and were never the first to do so, all soldiers of the RADC did very little in the way of any serious military exercises or training. Several times since transferring into the RADC other members of the Corps had told me they had served with me in units which I had never been anywhere near. One of these Corps members was Corporal Paul Buxton, otherwise known as BDP (Big Daft Paul). No amount of protestations would convince him that I had never served with him in the units he was talking about, he kept calling me an idiot because I couldn't remember him, I wouldn't mind but Paul only had an IQ of about seven. It was only when I met Steve on that training day that the penny dropped, we were both Full Corporals, dark haired, barrel chested, and both of us had moustaches that made us look like we had come out of the same womb at the same time. It was no wonder that Paul had mistaken me for Steve Roberts because we actually looked like twins; even though his mistake was understandable, it didn't change the fact that Paul Buxton was as thick as uncooked mince.

Steve was born in 1955 near Burton upon Trent and he had a criminal record from the age of 11 years old, but he wasn't actually convicted due to a lack of evidence. This was convenient for Steve because a conviction would have barred his enlistment into the Royal Pioneer Corps in 1977; Steve wanted to be a dog handler but as I've explained in 'Oath of Allegiance', Army Recruiters will only let you do what they and the British Army want you to do. He stayed in the RPC until he was forced to transfer into another Corps for his own benefit, a friend of his in the RPC was very ill and as a result went AWOL (Absent Without Leave) on a couple of occasions. Steve was a Regimental Policeman at the time and was privy to his friend being given a bit of a hard time by his regiment; so he wrote to Her Majesty the Queen explaining that his friends' treatment by the regiment was both cruel and unfair. Steve is the sort of friend who will always do what is right to defend a mate in trouble, even to the detriment of his own career. He got a reply from the Palace saying that they had passed his letter onto the Ministry of Defence who would hopefully be more adept at helping him with his conundrum. He was called into the

CSM's (Company Sergeant Major's) office and told he would be going on CO's (Commanding Officer's) Orders and charged with misconduct; the CSM guaranteed Steve that he would be busted on Orders and would soon be going to the Military Correction and Training Centre in Colchester, his military career would be over from the point of being marched in front of the Commanding Officer.

Fortunately for Steve the CO was on leave and so he was marched in front of Captain Moody the regimental 2nd in command; Captain Moody was a decent officer for whom Steve had done some baby-sitting. Much to the CSM's infuriation, Captain Moody laughed and called Steve a dickhead before telling him to fuck off out of his office; he told Steve that he was never to write to the queen again because she was a very busy lady. The CSM flew into a rage at the 2i/c's leniency and vented his anger on Steve before Captain Moody told him to calm down, the CSM then marched Steve out of the 2 i/c's office and after closing the door behind him he threatened Steve, "You had better put in for a transfer to another Corps because you are finished as far as I am concerned, I will personally see to it that you never get promoted in the Royal Pioneer Corps". Much to the annoyance of the CSM, Steve's first posting after transferring into the RADC was to the Dental Centre in the barracks where his old unit was based.

Steve always found trouble wherever he went and some of it was of his own making, at the RADC Depot was a Warrant Officer called Piles, a weedy snide of a 'man' who had enlisted directly into the RADC, Piles was the RQMS of the Depot and whilst Steve was on his initial dental training, he had the misfortune to have to work for Piles who treated him like a dogsbody. From the word go Steve and Piles hated each other's guts, Steve had to stand and listen to the RQMS tell him, "You are about to join the best Corps within the ranks of the British Army". That sort of bullshit was bad enough in Steve's eyes but when Piles ordered him to burn rubbish in the unit incinerator whilst it was pouring with rain, well, that just pushed Steve over the edge. Steve asked WO 2 Piles if the boxes of rubbish had been checked for combustible materials, Piles confirmed that he personally had checked each box and then confirmed it was all clear for burning; Steve carried the boxes to the incinerator after picking up a couple of large tins of alcohol from the RQMS's shelf. Steve threw the tins of explosive material into the incinerator along with the rubbish and retreated to a safe distance. The top of the incinerator flew up into the air and the explosion was heard throughout the depot, Piles and the RSM came running out of the main building to give Steve an almighty bollocking. Steve told the RSM that the RQMS had confirmed the rubbish had been cleared for burning and he also pointed out the fact that he had almost been killed as a result of Piles inefficiency. The RSM had no choice but to march Piles in front of the Commanding Officer to explain why the incident had happened and who was responsible for the destruction of his units' incinerator. Steve was completely exonerated by the Commanding Officer and Piles grew to hate Steve with a passion as a result of his Commanding Officers reprimand. It got to the stage where Steve had to have a quiet and personal chat with Piles to sort out their differences and although he hated Steve, Piles didn't have the guts to physically take him on; he always hid behind his senior rank.

As far as Steve was concerned, the best way to sort out a problem was to punch it straight in the face and that was what he used to do whilst moonlighting as a security guard from the RADC Dental Centre at Shorncliffe. He used to work at nights in the M20's motorway service station where unruly youths used to gather on a night time drinking cider and intimidating the customers. On one particular night Steve came up against three young men who thought they were real hard-men, Steve thought otherwise. They were all out of order and Steve tried to persuade them to move on explaining that it would be for the best, especially in regard to their own personal wellbeing. Oh the innocence of youth, they thought that three young men against one 'old man' was a no brainer, they expected Steve to back down and leave them to their own devices. By the time the police arrived one hard man was unconscious and the other two were a bit groggy as one had several teeth missing and the other had a broken jaw. As the Police radioed for an ambulance to attend at the incident they questioned Steve about the amount of force he had used to restrain the youths, it didn't look like he had actually used minimum force. When Steve pointed out the fact that there were three of them against just him, an 'old man', he had to deal with them quickly to make sure they didn't get him down on the floor, because if they did, they would then have given Steve a really good kicking. The Police said they would put in their report that the youths were very drunk and had fallen down the stairs before being arrested, they also told Steve that they wouldn't be able to cover up for him in future and he might consider using a little less violence the next time he came up against any sort of trouble.

The last time I saw Steve in our army days he was still moonlighting as a security guard but this time he was at the entrance of the Channel Tunnel in Folkestone whilst it was still under construction. I had been posted from Borden to the Dental Centre in Detmold in West Germany and just before my ferry left Dover I called in to see him at his security station. My old Ford Taunus car was loaded up to the gunnels with my ex-wife, our three children, a cat in one cage and a budgerigar in another, the poor kids were wedged in the back and surrounded by plastic carrier bags full of crap that my ex-wife felt she couldn't do without on the journey. Steve and I spent about five minutes saying goodbye and as he shook my hand he told me to keep in touch, but like a lot of things in life, reality prevents you from doing what you really should take the time to do.

It was over 25 years later that Steve contacted me on Facebook and invited me and Nicky out to his place in Spain where he and his partner Bernadette both teach English to young Spanish children. Steve met Bernadette whilst he was a Sergeant and running the Dental Centre at Shorncliffe. Although he hated his time in the RADC Steve openly admits that the only worthwhile thing he accomplished in his time in the Corps was meeting Bernadette, she was one of his civilian Dental Surgery Assistants and his life saviour. We spent the whole weekend at his house chatting about the old days, his teaching job and his recent punch up with a Spanish bloke who had driven into the back of his car. Steve! You really are a top man.

Corporal 'Cliff' Clifton RADC
I didn't spend much time with 'Cliff' during my service in the Royal Army Dental Corps, in fact we never even served

in the same Dental Group together, but we did accomplish good marks on a couple of courses we jointly attended . I did my DCA Class 1 Course at the RADC Depot in Aldershot with him and the JMQC (Junior Military Qualification Course) Course at the RAMC Depot in Ash Vale. All RADC 'Other Ranks' had to do their military promotion courses with the RAMC at the medics' depot in Ash Vale near Aldershot. 'Cliff' had originally enlisted in the British Army into his local Infantry Regiment, the Sherwood Foresters (Nottinghamshire and Derbyshire Regiment), but for the benefit of his wife and his family life; he decided to transfer into the RADC for a more settled army life.

'Cliff' was a good looking fair haired and physically very fit young man, he and I went for a few pints one night during our DCA 1 Course in Aldershot, we went up to a unit bar at 22 Field Hospital RAMC. The place was buzzing when we arrived and although we were slightly inebriated, compared to the majority of the medics in the bar who were pissed out of their tiny skulls, 'Cliff' and I could almost be classified as sober. We found a quiet part of the bar and started chatting to some of the medics we assumed were from 22 Field Hospital; 'Cliff' and I were eventually pinned into a corner of the room by six particular medics, one of whom was an RAMC Physical Training Instructor who turned out to be a real gobshite. Who would have believed it, someone in the British Army who was employed to beast other soldiers on training runs, turns out to be a motor mouth who didn't know his arse from his elbow. I studied the other medics around us as the gobshite started poking and taunting 'Cliff', the one on my left was so drunk that he was pouring his pint of lager down his chin and chest while instinctively swallowing as if the alcohol was going down his throat, the other two next to him were laughing at their PTI hero as he continued to mock my drinking partner. I felt the other five medics were a bit in awe of their PTI mate and were looking up to him, if he kicked off then the others would simply follow his example and kick the crap out of me and 'Cliff'. The PTI kept goading 'Cliff' about what unit we were both from and 'Cliff' sensibly told him we were from 16 Field Ambulance RAMC down in Mons Barracks, if we told them we were in the same Corps as them we might avoid getting into a fight. The PTI suddenly snarled, "Well fancy that, you're both from 16 Field Ambulance are you. Me and my mates here, are also from 16 Field Ambulance and yet we've never fucking seen you down in Mons Barracks, how do a couple of wankers like you two explain that fact"! SHIT! We'd been rumbled and it was starting to get ugly, and I don't just mean the faces of the six disagreeable drunks, they were all looking to give me and 'Cliff' a good stomping. The fact that me and 'Cliff' were Gob Doctors wasn't going to help our cause either, that would only encourage our tormentors even further. I looked at the medic on the far left and thought, 'I can push his pint glass into his face, knee the one next to him in the bollocks and then stick the nut on the third one, 'Cliff' will be able to handle the other three without even breaking into a sweat'. The gobshite PTI then started pushing 'Cliff' and telling him that he could run him into the ground, as a PTI, he said he would be able to knock ten bells of crap out of him. 'Cliff' told the PTI to, "Go and take your face for a shit, I've jumped over tougher and bigger men than you just to get into a fight, you're definitely small fry"!

I turned to 'Cliff' and said, "Leave it mate, if we get into a scrap and get locked up, we'll both be RTU'd (Returned To Unit) off the course and I don't know about you but I need the extra money that the course will bring in". I think 'Cliff was eager to start punching someone but the thought of his family going short just for the pure satisfaction of knocking the stuffing out of this windbag, didn't make any sense. The windbag then turned to me and said, "Shut it fat man or I'll take you out for a run, you could do with losing a few pounds". I felt my anger rise, this loudmouth definitely needed a smack in his very big gob, 'Cliff' grab my wrist and clenched fist and said, "Leave it Harry, remember what you just said about getting RTU'd mate". The confrontation ended when 'Cliff' finally lost his rag and shouted at the PTI, "Right fuckface! Outside now! I'm about to teach you a lesson you'll never forget"! The PTI bottled it as soon as 'Cliff' grabbed him by the throat and he started bleating, "Alright mate, calm down… you clearly can't take joke". After refusing the PTI's offer to buy us a pint, (I think 'Cliff' hinted about where the PTI could stick his pints of lager), 'Cliff' and I departed the bar with the intention of returning back to our own barracks. As we walked out of the main entrance 'Cliff' was still seething, on the left hand side of the door was a small metal and wood ornamental bench on which sat a paratrooper with his latest conquest. We were walking past the bench when the Para, who was wearing a maroon sweatshirt with a Depot Para logo on it, shouted, "Fucking Crap Hats"! 'Cliff' moved like lightning, I swear to you, I have never seen another man move as quick in my entire life, he charged towards the bench whilst screaming like a banshee on speed. He punched the Para in the face and with his forward momentum he bulldozed the bench over backwards knocking the Para and his new found girlfriend onto their backs. The whole night was obviously going to end in a very undignified manner, particularly for the Para's girlfriend who flashed her knickers at me as she tumbled over backwards, she seemed to be stuck on her back and waggled her legs in the air to try and get upright again. I can still see 'Cliff' punching the Para over and over again as blood started to pour from the Airborne Warriors nose and mouth, his new sweetheart was screaming her head off at the shock and speed of the violence, she was making an awful lot of noise compared to her lover who was now as quiet as a Trappist Monk.

I pulled 'Cliff' off the now unconscious Para and shouted, "For fuck's sake, leave him 'Cliff'". We both stood up and started running down Gunn Hill before making our way back to our accommodation, 'Cliff' and I were both laughing like a couple of homicidal maniacs all the way back. In the morning we spotted the PTI from the night before sitting in the dental clinical wing reception waiting to be seen by one of our dentists, he had a big fat lip and was missing one of his front teeth. At closing time in the bar the night before, 22 Field Hospitals' RSM (Regimental Sergeant Major) accompanied the Orderly Sergeant on his night-time checks of making sure the NAAFI bar was closed on time. The gobby PTI took it upon himself to tell the RSM to, "Piss off out of our bar; you have no right to be in here". The RSM disputed the claim by punching him straight in the mouth". At least my mate 'Cliff' displayed a bit more self-discipline than the RAMC Regimental Sergeant Major, having said that I think the gobby PTI got off lightly, if 'Cliff' had set about him he would have been waking up in the Cambridge Military Hospital, probably in the bed next to a recently beaten up Paratrooper from the Airborne Depot.

I have never seen 'Cliff' since we completed both of our courses together and it was such a brief window of time that we spent in each other's company, yet in that small time frame 'Cliff' made a huge impression on me. The Royal Army Dental Corps should feel honoured that these two men, and all the other TFI's, (Transfer In's) who served within their ranks, for transferring into their Corps, they made it a better and more interesting formation in which to serve.

AS A CIVIL SERVANT

As a Civil Servant I'm not sure where to begin with what must have been the most mind-numbing and unsatisfying parts of my adult working life. That's not to say my life and work as an Accommodation Services Accountant wasn't funny, because at times it was unequivocally hilarious. You'll probably know that the Ministry of Defence recruits and trains a massive amount of drones who are released into the wilderness of the Civil Service. Once trained, they can be heard constantly whingeing and whining as they wander aimlessly through the corridors of many Military camps saying, "I don't care what you say; I can't do anything without a number three copy of an AFG 1033. And make sure it's been signed and rubber stamped by the Regimental Quartermaster or I won't action it!" I have heard many serving soldiers comment about civvies working for them, "What a bloody waste of time, how the hell are we supposed to get anything done when that stuck up cow keeps sticking her neb into where it's not wanted. She should be under some sort of care in the community order!" The worst of these human psychological 'car-crashes' were usually allowed to govern at the top of our particular management system in the ASU (Accommodation Services Unit) world, and to make things even worse, the majority of them came from within the ranks of the British Army. These strutting and arrogant ex Officers and Warrant Officers all fell into one of the following categories, they were either catastrophically inept or they were a bullshitting bully, in a lot of cases they managed to be both, one thing was for sure, they would never, ever, have maintained a successful career outside of the MOD. For the purposes of this book I shall only be telling you about the cretins I have personally observed, but I'll also tell you about some of the wonderful and hardworking people who were an absolute pleasure to work alongside, not all Civil Servants are lethargic sloths.

After leaving the army my first job interview was at Imphal Barracks in York, the Civil Service vacancy was for a post as an Accommodation Services Accountant. The job would involve me moving soldiers and their families into and out of their allocated Married Quarters, in the event of any damages to the ASU furniture, or if the house wasn't clean enough when they were moving out, I would raise the appropriate bills. The ASU unit I would be working for was commanded and controlled by the Royal Army Ordnance Corps and a lot of the senior management who were on my interview board were ex-blanket stackers (RAOC). An ex Warrant Officer Class 1 from this Corps also applied for the same job vacancy as me, unsurprisingly he got the job and he pipped me at the post purely because he was wearing the correct Corps tie on his interview. When the winning applicant was told that he would be starting on about £10,500 a year (This was in 1993) he threw his teddy in the corner of the room and told the board, "I wouldn't get out of bed for that kind of money, I'm looking for a job that will bring in about 64K a year." Cue telephone call to Harry Clacy telling him "We thought you were excellent on the interview and we would like to offer you the post of ASA 31 in Imphal Barracks York." Having done my research about the job I already knew how piss poor the wages were, and as I was qualified to do naff all else, I was more than happy to get out of bed for £10,500 a year. What you are about to read are the true but probably implausible stories about my shitty life as a Civil Servant.

RUTH AND THE DICKHEADS

To be honest the job of an ASA wasn't exactly taxing in any way shape or form, but when starting any new employment it can be quiet nerve wracking until you learn the ropes. When I got to my office on the first day I found out that Mrs Ruth Whitely was the lady who would be working with me, she was the storekeeper of our MQES (Married Quarters Exchange Store). Ruth looked after the stock of light bulbs, toilet brushes, hoover bags and other free detritus we exchanged for the forces families living in our Married Quarters in York. Ruth was about 5ft 4 ins tall, or should I say, 5 ft 4 ins short, her grey hair was also short and although she was small in height, she was big in heart. Ruth was about ten years older than me and was a Yorkshire woman through and through; if you didn't want to hear the real answer to a problem then, "you shouldn't ask tut bluoody question in't fost place." The other ASA who shared our two offices and large store area was Wally Fryer, he definitely wouldn't beat Ruth in a height race. Wally was an ex RCT soldier just like me but was only five years off retirement; he was a cheerful and friendly enough sort of chap but was prone to depressive moods and could be capricious if things weren't going his way.

Ruth was more instrumental in teaching me about my new job than Wally who was in charge, with over twenty year's of experience as an ASA he was totally NFI (Not Flipping Interested). He wanted to be posted to the ASU office at the Defence School of Transport in Leconfield, Wally's house was also in Leconfield and it would take him less than two minutes to get out of bed and into the office as opposed to the hour long drive it took him to get to York. The problem with getting a posting within the ASU world was that the whole system worked on a dead mans shoes basis, I worked with Walley for about two years before one of the poor bastards at Leconfield eventually popped his clogs and Walley got his inter-unit move.

I attended about three Move in/ Move out's under the guidance of another ASA before I was allowed to go solo, and before we go on, you have to understand that ASA's were disliked by most Forces families on Move in/Move out's and for several reasons. Firstly they were pedantic about the cleanliness of Married Quarters when a Serviceman moved out, mainly because the incoming occupant would always tell us, "You expect me to move into a filthy shit hole like this; my wife and I have just handed over an immaculate quarter in Germany" (everyone's previous bloody Married Quarter was always, allegedly, left in an immaculate state). And secondly, a lot of ASA's, even though they were now civilians, continued to strut around like they were still in charge of an Infantry Company. Some of them also treated the occupants with contempt and talked to them as if they were shit on the bottom of their shoes. A lot of ex-servicemen can't let it go. For these reasons some Move in/Move out's could be tetchy affairs and so was the case on my very first appointment under the guidance of Bob, an ASA based at Strensall. Bob was a bullish ex-infantry man who was nearing retirement, but at every opportunity he addressed and instructed "you people" on what and how he wanted things to be done. This man lacked any kind of social grace whatsoever.

The Move in was at Hollis Crescent in Strensall and the soldier moving in was a Corporal in the Royal Signals who was posted into 2 Signal Regiment in Fulford Barracks in York. On inspection of the Married Quarters cooker, the young Corporal looked in the oven and found traces of baked on carbon on one of the metal shelves. He took Bob to task, "This cooker is minging, if I had left my cooker in Germany like this I would have been given a bill, you will have to get your cleaners to come back and re-clean the whole cooker before I move in here." Unfortunately that was like a personal slap in the face for my senior partner in Married Quarter cleanliness, Bob wasn't going to be spoken too in that manner, and certainly not by a "bloody jumped up Corporal in the Royal Signals". Ironically my guardian angel of an ASA spoke to the Corporal without any recognition of his own hypocrisy, "Now you listen to me Corporal, you people come into my garrison and start laying down the law on something you know nothing about and expect preferential treatment. This cooker is perfectly clean by my own personal standards and is therefore more than acceptable for you and your wife. I suggest, Corporal, you get off your high horse and sign this Handover/Takeover certificate and stop wasting my very valuable time." The Royal Signals Corporal was very tired and irritable having travelled overnight from Germany by car; he was having none of it, "Don't speak to me in that manner, where the hell do you get off talking to people like that, the cooker is dirty and I want your cleaner to come back and get this oven up to my standard of cleanliness."

I watched the pontificating fly back and forth like a verbal tennis match as both sides got louder and more pig-headed, it got to the point where Eddie Gallagher, the FHWS (Families Housing and Welfare Services) representative and I tried to intervene and calm things down. The ASA finally ripped the arms, legs and head off his metaphorical teddy bear and threw it in the corner of the room; he put the house file and all the house keys in his briefcase, slammed the lid shut and shouted, "Right! Out, now! I am now officially cancelling this March in. Corporal! You and your family can now drive down to Garbutt House in York and report to the Housing Commandant where you can bang your tabs in. We'll soon see what he has to say about this!" We all trooped outside and got into our cars and drove the eight miles back to Fulford in York where Bob and his incoming occupant reported to Lieutenant Colonel (Retired) Hodgetts MBE. Ted Hodgetts had served in the Green Howards infantry Regiment for nearly thirty years; he had risen from the rank of Private all the way up to Lieutenant Colonel and was Regimental Quartermaster of his Battalion before taking the job of Quartermaster at RMA (Royal Military Academy) Sandhurst. He was a Middlesbrough man who was ferociously proud of his regiment and his beloved Middlesbrough FC; he was also dismissive about all other arms of the British Army with some tongue in cheek ridicule. Ted was a man's man and after listening to both sides of the story he asked the Royal Signals Corporal to drive back up to the Married Quarter and wait for Bob, after the Corporal had left Ted then told Bob to grow up and stop behaving like a spoilt child. He pointed out that the soldier had travelled a long way and the best thing to do would have been to make a note of the complaint, give his cleaner an hours pay to get the job done properly and move on with the rest of his life. Ted didn't have the time or inclination to sort out childish squabbles between ASA's and occupants of Married Quarters.

After Bob and his disgruntled incoming occupant left Ted's office I went back to my office in the same building to have a chat with Ruth. I asked her if all ASA's were this confrontational on Move-ins and Move-outs of Married Quarters, with her natural Yorkshire wit she told me, "With Bob? Yes, I'm afraid they are my love, Wally is less aggressive but can be confrontational if pushed." I asked about Jeff the ASA over at Driffield. "Now then…let me tell you my love, he is totally different from the rest of them… he starts and ends all Move Ins and Move Outs looking for a squabble. Still, you get used to it after a while, I find that all ASA's can be real drama queens and they are generally dickheads." Ruth was a down to earth and honest pint sized font of ASU knowledge.

After working with Ruth for about a year she noticed I was staying later and later at work, it wasn't as a result of my work load because you could have taught a monkey to become an ASA, and the primate would probably have done a better job, and for just a handful of bananas. The reason I was staying later and later every day was because I didn't want to go home, I had been married for about twenty years to a woman whose only requirements in holy matrimony was: a. that her husband provide a roof over her head and fill the larder with plenty of food, and b. that she didn't have to provide the aforementioned husband with any physical or emotional support, comfort and warmth within any given 24 hour period. I was both lonely and sexually frustrated; and in all honesty I had been like this for many years. Ruth could tell I wasn't happy and I think she felt sorry for me, she had met Ronnie on a few occasions and being the shrewd woman that she was, I think Ruth was suspicious of all Ronnie's true motives. I hadn't even mentioned my home life to her and yet she had sensed my trepidation about going home. Over the coming weeks I started to reveal to Ruth exactly why I was gloomy when the clock struck home time, as I put my coat on she would say to me, "Ah bless you love, you don't want to go home do you?" I told Ruth that I was seriously thinking about booking an appointment with a solicitor and initiating divorce proceedings against Ronnie, for twenty years I had emotionally propped her up and it was now becoming tiresome, her mood swings were starting to make me angry. Ruth was brutally honest about my predicament, "No-one else can sort this out for you, you're a big boy and you have to sort out your own problems." She asked me if I felt anything for Ronnie and the truth was the only feelings I had were ones of animosity. "Well, you know what you have to do then pet, you have to make that first step and visit a solicitor, neither I nor anyone else is going to step up and fix this for you, you need to get off your arse and do it yourself." Harsh but true words and I've never forgotten them, Ruth was absolutely right and she alone gave me the mental nudge that I needed to do what had to be done for the sake of my own sanity. I booked an appointment with Phillip Hamer solicitors in Hull and started the divorce ball rolling, my son Matt was 26 years old and serving in the Royal Air Force at the time, my daughter Naomi was married to a Warrant Officer serving in the Adjutant Generals Corps, and Daniel was at college in Bridlington learning how to be a chef. I have loved Matt, Naomi and Daniel from the first time I clapped eyes on them and feel the same way today, I don't consider Matt and Naomi my step-children because as far as I'm concerned they have always been my son and daughter. Having said that, I felt the time was right for me to unburden myself from Ronnie, but not from them.

This all happened about twenty years ago but I have never forgotten my debt to Ruth, since divorcing Ronnie I have met and married Nicky, the most beautiful woman in the world, a woman who loves me unconditionally, a woman who is neither selfish nor paranoid. A woman who believes in me and when she told me to write a book and that people would find it funny, she was right, as a result of her imagination and forethought I'm now writing this, my third book. I have been married to my wife Nicky for five years now and she has negated everything I went through in the twenty years I was married to Ronnie, but if it wasn't for Ruth, I don't like to think where I would be now. I would publicly like to thank two of the most amazing women I have ever met in my life, Ruth Whitley and Nicky Clacy.

RETINAL SCREENING

It was only when Walley had eventually moved to Leconfield that Ruth and I could start training up his replacement, an ASA who was an ex-Coldstream Guardsman, or as he liked to tell anyone gullible enough to listen to his semi-posh voice, "Whilst serving in the Coldstream Guards I was promoted to the position of Senior Drum Major of the whole of the Household Division." He was a very polite, pompous and incredibly smart man who had been brainwashed in all the usual British Army Foot Guards traditions, "If it moves and has pips on its shoulder, then salute it, and if it doesn't move or have any pips, polish the damned thing!" Our brand-new ASU colleague automatically fell into the familiar format of most ex-Warrant Officer ASA's, he spontaneously assumed command (even though he knew nothing about the job) and he also presumed Ruth and I were going to personally work for him. Every day he expected Ruth to clear all the stockpiled new toilet brushes and holders off the shelves in the store, she then had to thoroughly dust each shelf and evenly line them all up again in three ranks.

Our new ASA was so institutionalised by the British Army that he made a compliments slip for himself that he would paper-clip to any correspondence he may have to send in the post, the slip included a silhouetted picture of a Coldstream Guards Drum Major wearing a Bearskin and carrying a 6 foot Drum Mace. Next to the figure he listed his ASU address, contact telephone and fax numbers and it also noted that he was an ex-Senior Drum Major of the Household Division (like anyone ever got the chance to forget). This compliments slip was a work of art and it had had taken the 'new boy' over a week to draw and titivate up to his necessary standards of perfection. The compliments slip only needed a couple of finishing touches and it would be ready to go for print, by that I mean it was ready to be taken up the corridor to the Family Housing and Welfare Services photocopier, and my understudy would then spend the next hour or so fannying around so he could get six copies of his compliment slip onto one piece of A4 paper. Whilst this new ASA went on a Move out he rather foolishly left his nearly completed compliments slip on his desk where it could be viewed by all and sundry that came in and out of our building.

Up the corridor in the Family Housing and Welfare Department worked Kevin Redman who was also an ex-infantryman, but he had served in the Kings Regiment, soldiers from this regiment were recruited from Manchester and Liverpool and they all hated anyone who was serving, or had served, within any of the 'posh' Guards Regiments. 'Kev' was a 'Scouser' through and through and when wearing a trilby hat he looked the absolute spit of Frank Sinatra. 'Kev' was always in our part of the building taking the mickey and making everyone laugh, he constantly had a cup of coffee in one hand and a lit cigarette in the other, he saw the compliments slip on the desk and shouted, "Wot der fok is dat, is e' avin a fokin laff or woh. Dat bloke is so fahr oop is own arse ee can't see fokin daylight". My telephone started ringing and as I went to answer it I heard Ruth say to Kev, "Don't mess about with it Kev, he will go flipping mad, he's been working on that thing all week". As I dealt with my phone call I could hear the pair of them laughing and giggling like a couple of adolescent school kids. I hung up the phone after my caller had rung off and 'Kev' came past my desk chuckling and said, "Right, I'm off ar lah, see you later 'arry", he seemed to be in a rush to get back to his own office. At the same time I heard the new ASA coming through the main entrance on the other side of the store and he looked quizzically at Ruth as she was trying to stifle her own laughter. He stood up to his immaculate 6ft 4inches and bristled as he assumed that he was again the butt of yet another joke, his lack of a sense of humour meant he could laugh at anything but himself and the Coldstream Guards. He put his briefcase on his desk and noticed that someone had been tampering with his compliments slip, I heard him shout, "For God's sake, who the bloody hell has done that"! I approached his desk and looked at the slip in his hand, 'Kev' had snowpake'd the top of the silhouetted Drum Majors mace, and on the top of the 6 foot staff he had drawn a bass broom head so the Drum Major looked like a road sweeper.

I eventually followed Walley down to Leconfield when I was posted to Normandy Barracks, this time an ASA had actually retired and not popped his clogs. It was sad for me to leave Ruth because we had a lot of fun working together and it was her alone who gave me the courage, and the kick up the arse that I needed to initiate divorce proceedings against Ronnie, she also helped me furnish the misappropriated Married Quarter in York that I was living in after I had moved out of the matrimonial home. After moving jobs to Leconfield I ultimately moved into a rented house with Nicky when I finally realised that she liked me, it took her over 18 months to amass the courage to let me know and another 6 months before we found a place to rent. We moved into a cosy two bedroomed house in Morton Lane which was a stone's throw away from Beverley town centre and just a couple of miles drive from Leconfield camp where I was now going to work.

I moved into the office next to Walley in Accommodation Stores which was closely linked with the Quartermasters Department of DST (Defence School of Transport). The building was also the office of the military manager in Accommodation Stores, Staff Sergeant Jed McGinley RLC, a hard bitten Glaswegian equipped with a razor sharp wit and kitbags full of sarcasm. He had several members of staff working for him, one of which was his Senior Store keeper Colin Handley, a short-sighted 5 foot 11 inch, barrel chested, Yorkshire leviathan of a man with hands the size of shovels, to be honest I think Colin makes Shrek look like George Clooney. He was even quicker witted than his boss Jed, and about three thousand times more sarcastic, if Colin liked you he would move heaven and earth to sort out a problem for you; if he disliked you he wouldn't waste his time pissing over your prostrate dead body. One other point about Colin is the fact that he can skilfully lie to an incredible standard, he could tell you that the moon is made out of Gouda cheese and you would probably bet on your own life that it was true.

Just up the road from Accommodation Stores was the Quartermasters Department where a whole host of QM staff worked, one of the staff who worked there was the Technical Quartermaster Captain MacMordie, an Irishman who had completed over 30 years of service within the British Army, he was now serving as a retired officer at DST Leconfield. With over 30 years' service Captain 'Mac' had seen the film, read the book, and acted in the play, there wasn't much you could tell him and it would be even harder to pull the wool over his eyes. At one point in his career he was a WO 1 RSM (Regimental Sergeant Major), and no-one can lie to them without beads of sweat dripping from the forehead.

Colin was down at the QM's one day whilst I was off having my annual Retinal Screening; all diabetics should have this examination done at least once a year. The examiners put atropine drops in each eye so the pupils dilate and they can take a photograph of the back of each eye and examine the patients' retina, the photographs can then be read by a doctor back at the hospital to determine how the diabetics' insulin management is progressing. Regular screening of the eyes can avoid a diabetic from going blind by adjusting their insulin regime and/or diet; if they start having retinal problems then laser treatment will stop a retinal bleed and hopefully arrest the fault from progressing. Having atropine drops in the eyes can sting quite badly and does affect a person's vision for about six hours during which the patient can't legally drive a car during that period of time, I therefore usually took the whole day off work when I was having a retinal screening examination. Captain 'Mac' bumped into Colin whilst he was in the QM's department and he mentioned that I wasn't answering my telephone that morning; he enquired if I was on leave. Colin told him where I was and that he would get me to contact him on my return the following day. I didn't know that Colin had mischievously told Captain 'Mac' that I was having rectal screening and not retinal screening. In the morning I went down to see Captain 'Mac' and we had the following conversation in his office:

Captain 'Mac': "Ah good morning Harry, come on in and take a seat".

(I didn't sit down because I was in a bit of a hurry to attend a Move Out in the next 20 minutes).

Me: "I won't sit down but thank you anyway, how are you today"?

Captain 'Mac': "I'm fine, but more importantly how are you (he tilted his head to one side and seemed to be nodding at something behind my waist), I notice you haven't…you know…sat down. How did your…you know…screening go"?

He continued to nod at something behind me and I was starting to get a little confused at his strange behaviour.

Me: "Yeah, it went alright, they couldn't find anything wrong but it's best to get everything checked out just in case I start bleeding (Captain 'Mac' seemed to wince at this point). I tell you what, it's really difficult to keep your eye open wide enough when they are having a really good look inside, (Now a look of disgust appeared on the face of Captain 'Mac') I'm also uncomfortable with having someone's face that close to me whilst they are trying to take a photograph of it."

Captain 'Mac': "Good God man, have you…you know…bled from there before"?

Me: "No I haven't but they tell me you can become blind if you do though."

Captain 'Mac': "Jesus no, well I never knew that, would you credit it"?

Me: "I was given some stuff to help the examination but it just made my eyes water, it really bloody hurts you know."

Captain 'Mac': "I can imagine, what the bloody hell did they use?"

Me: "It was atropine drops and I had to lean over the back of a chair whilst they put them in, it was very uncomfortable and I felt a bit dizzy afterwards."

Captain 'Mac': "Still, if you felt dizzy, I suppose it was lucky that you already had your head down between your legs then".

It was at this point that I started to realise that Captain 'Mac' and I were having different conversations.

Me: "I've had retinal screening done for my diabetes, the NHS annually check out the retina's at the back of my eyes, what the hell do you think I've had examined"! Captain 'Mac' looked relieved and started laughing.

Captain 'Mac': "Colin told me you were having your arse looked at yesterday".

COMMANDANT'S CURTAINS

We had a rest room in the accommodation stores at Leconfield that was furnished with comfy sofa's, armchairs, kettle, brew kit, toaster, fridge, freezer and a colour television set with DVD player, other than these begged, borrowed and stolen items of creature comforts, we really roughed it in our place of work. At 10 o'clock on the nail every morning one of our staff (usually me) would put the kettle on and start toasting the bread, bagels, crumpets or muffins ready to have lashings of butter and peanut-butter applied. Apparently, over two hundred meters away at the Regimental Headquarters, the noise of our arteries hardening disturbed the Commandants' morning nap.

It was during our morning tea breaks that Dylan, one of our store-keepers, would enthral us all with his latest tale of woe, Dylan was a depressing West Yorkshire soothsayer who had served in the RAF as a store-man for about twelve years. He was now 55 years old and continued with his scintillating career as a store-keeper but this time as a civilian, (after all those years in the RAF you'd think he would have been somewhat of an expert at store-keeping, but he wasn't) he was also an avid Manchester United supporter. His anecdotes were legendary and always followed the same format; he was like a verbal Death-eater who sucked the very life out of you. On this particular morning he enthralled us with, "Hey oop Colin, me and Fran went shoppin int Tesco tuther week, now when wor it, I think it wor on't Monday, or wor it on't Wednesday, I can't really remember, anyway, what day it were on, dun't really matter but I do think it wor on't Wednesday. No! I tell you what, it wor on't Monday, I've remembered now coz Man yew wor playin in't cup game against Leeds 'White Shite' United, Giggsy med a belter of a ghoal, he took tut ball from ar area and ran all tut way oop the left wing before crossing the purfect ball, Dimitar Berbatov couldn't fookin miss, it were a bullet of an edder.

Anyway that's all irrelevant, worrah were goin ter tell yer woz, now hang on a minute, it weren't onna Monday, it were on a foockin Wednesday, Man yew were playing in't Champions League game against Bayern Munich, Man yew were so bludy unlucky mate, we shood ave scored an 'at full, if it weren't fer their keeper we would have been four oop at arf time, bloody Keano played a blinder, onestly Col, ee played art of is skin, anyway, that's all irrelevant, worrah were goin ter tell yer were, bugger me, now ar coom ter think abart it, it worrah Monday." By this stage of the story we were all losing the will to live as Dylan droned on and on, he eventually arrived at the destination of his story and told us that Tesco was having a sale on Budweiser beers and it would be worth Colin's while buying some. Dylan was one boring Civil Servant. Two weeks after telling us this tedious story he came into work and mentioned to Colin, "You remember tuther week when ar were tellin you abarht them Budweisers on sale at Tesco's, yewer not goin ter believe this, it worrah Wednesday when me and Fran went."

During one of these epic mid-morning orations the phone rang in the office and we all jumped out of our comfy chairs and shouted in unison, "I'll get it, no leave it to me, you stay here and listen to Dylan's story"! Whoever got out of the restroom door first won the prize of answering the telephone, the others had to sit back down and continue listening to Dylan prattle on. On this particular occasion I got out of the door first and made a wanking sign to Colin as I left the room of gloom. I answered the phone and the RQMS (Regimental Quartermaster Sergeant) asked me if I would meet him over at the Commandants office to measure it up for some new curtains, the existing ones were looking old and worn and the full Colonel was expecting a VIP visitor soon and he demanded that they be replaced. I went back to Dylan's Dominion of Dullness and rescued my mate Colin, "Come on Col, we've got to go and measure up the Commandant for some new curtains." Colin jumped at the chance to get away from yet another of Dylan's tedious proclamations, "OK" he said, "Let's hope the Commandant can at last pull himself together." We gathered the curtain samples, tape measure, notepad and pen and set off for DST's Headquarters to meet the Quartermasters Senior Warrant Officer.

The Commandant didn't have an Admin Assistant or Secretary, oh no, he had what was called a Personal Assistant who was often referred to as the 'Commandants PA'. His 'PA' at the time was a bitter and twisted divorcee called Siobhan and she believed that she was the gate-keeper of the Commandants office, she alone held the golden key that was needed to unlock the entrance to the chief wizard of Leconfield, no-one passed through her office and into the wonderland of the Commandants office without her permission. She fended off unworthy visitors and lesser mortals to guard him and his office as if they were her own personal possessions. I didn't share her point of view and so I walked straight through her office, said "Good Morning" and then walked into the Commandant's office after knocking on his door, Joan was out from behind her desk quicker than an RCT Driver could sink a pint of Amstel beer. She wailed as I bravely strode onwards, "Come back! You can't go in there." Clearly I could go in there because I had already got in there.

The Commandant was a bull of a man with very short and balding grey hair; he looked up from the paperwork on his desk and rather rudely shouted, "What do you want!" The Seventh Cavalry, in the form of Siobhan, arrived just a bit behind me, Colin and the RQMS. She started bleating, "I'm so sorry Colonel, they just barged in without my permission." I set out my stall immediately and as I offered the curtain samples to him I told the Commandant, "I believe you want some new curtains for your office Colonel, I am the man who can make your drape dreams come true." He stood up from behind his desk and arrogantly waved his hand in my face saying, "My PA does that sort of thing so you'll have to deal with her, Siobhan, take them into your office and choose whatever curtains you think would be suitable for my office." Somewhat put out at the rejection of my personal services to this mediocrity of a British Army Semi-Senior Officer, I tossed the samples at Siobhan and said, "Here you are sweetheart, take these through to your office and choose the Colonel some nice looking curtain's will you. Unfortunately Colonel we don't have any records of the sizes of your office windows (this was a down-right lie on my part but I was getting a bit miffed by his condescending attitude and I wanted to give him a bit of pay-back) so I'll have to measure you up now if that's alright?" The old boy was also starting to get a bit miffed and barked, "Can't you come back later when I'm not here?" To my eternal shame and delight, I lied again, "Sorry Colonel, but unlike you I'm a very busy man, either I measure you up now or you may have to wait another couple of months before I can come back." I stepped forward and proceeded to climb on his desk which had a window immediately to the side of it, "We might as well get this out of the way for you now Colonel, it saves me wasting my very valuable time having to come back and do you again later, Colin, have you got the tape measure mate?"

The RQMS went cold, clammy and very pale in the face as he stood like a rabbit suddenly caught in the headlights of a very fast car, he was a soldier who hopefully still had a military career ahead of him and he wanted to get all the way up to Regimental Sergeant Major, I was probably putting his promotion chances at risk because he would be deemed to be guilty by my very obnoxious association. Colin handed me the tape measure and stood next to the desk ready to write down the measurements I called out. I hung the lipped edge of the tape measure on the curtain rail and pulled the tape down to just over the edge of the window sill to get the drop size needed for the curtain, as I bent over I deliberately shoved my over-sized arse in the Commandants face. Colin told me later that the Colonel recoiled in horror and revulsion at the spectacle of my posterior that was about 6 inches from his face. Before getting the chance to take the width size of the window; the Commandants phone started to ring and I instinctively gently kicked it towards him saying, "Answer that Colonel, and if it's for me tell them I'm not here." As he took the call I made a nuisance of myself taking the other window's measurements. After hanging up the phone the Commandant suddenly snarled, "Haven't you finished yet, I've got lots of things that need my immediate attention." As I stepped off the leather armchair underneath the main window in the office, I let rip with a fart that shook the very foundations of the building we were standing in, I scratched my balls and said to the Commandant, "Sorry about that Colonel but I had a wicked 'Ruby Murray' last night, give me a call if you need anything else." Colin tried to stifle his laughter as Siobhan covered her nose and we all tramped out of the office. If you treat me like an ignoramus lout I tend to behave like one.

NUISANCE PHONE CALLS

I moved office from the Accommodation Stores because the new Quartermaster thought I was a disruptive influence on his staff. The QM believed that Colin Handley, one of his Senior Storekeepers, didn't have The Defence School of Transport's interests at heart and he questioned his loyalty to the unit, he believed Colin should be trying to get one over on the ASU to avoid DST having to pay any bills for damages and deficiencies. Colin and I did get on extremely well and even though I worked for ASU 2 Division and he came under DST Leconfield; we both worked together for the good and benefit of everyone concerned. Our working relationship was based on total honesty and trust with each other at all times. I did raise bills against DST for damages and deficiencies but on quite a few occasions I let things slide and wrote equipment off when I shouldn't have, I did this purely because Colin asked me to do it as a favour for DST. As far as I was concerned we were all pissing out of the same pot anyway and to bill DST for stolen cutlery from the Junior Ranks Mess seemed a pointless exercise, any bill I raised took money from DST's budget but we all worked for the same firm. After the SQMS told Colin of the QM's disappointment in his imagined treachery, Colin said, "Right, the QM can go fuck himself from now on, I have dug him and this unit out of the shit on many occasions, Harry, from this point onwards you can raise bills for everything and I won't ask you for any favours for the unit. Let's see what he thinks the next time Harry gives him a huge bill." The QM didn't like it when I raised monthly bills of over £3000 for knives forks and spoons that had been stolen from the Junior Ranks Mess, the Sergeants Mess, and yes, even from those most honourable of gentlemen in the Officers Mess. Even British Army Officers are thieving toe-rags when they want to eat a pot noodle in the comfort of their room at night. The bill for the Officers Mess 'misappropriated' EPNS cutlery, was taken as a personal vendetta by the Quartermaster.

Moving me to another office just compounded the problems for the Quartermaster because Colin now had to come over to my office on the other side of camp to sort out any problems DST had with the ASU side of business. Colin now spent most of his time out of the Accommodation Stores office and more time on the other side of camp in mine. I was given an office in the Defence Housing Executive complex that was located in an old Married Quarter, Mrs Anita Wain kindly agreed to let me have one of the rooms upstairs as long as I consented not to be a disruptive influence on her and her admin assistant Audrey Middlemass. I agreed but didn't keep my word; Audrey was just a pint-sized bundle of Scottish fun and one day whilst it was pouring with rain I picked her up with one arm and locked her out in the back garden where we worked. She roared with laughter as she jumped up and down in mock fury outside the kitchen window as she became drenched in the downpour. Anita and Audrey had the downstairs offices whilst I and another DHE officer used the upstairs ones, we all shared the kitchen downstairs to stand around at 10 o'clock (I'm a civilian now so I don't have to call it 1000 hours) and have a cup of coffee.

One particular day not long after I had moved into my new residence, Colin came over with a list of damages and deficiencies that need sorting out and as usual we had a coffee in the kitchen before starting business. I had just started to make the hot beverages when the phone in my office upstairs started ringing; it is one of my personal traits that I have to answer a phone if it is ringing. I turned to Colin and said, "Sorry mate, I'll just have to get that, can you finish making the brews for me?" He did his usual comedy act of complaining about having to do everything for everyone in Leconfield Camp. I ran up the stairs and picked up the phone, "Good morning, you are through to Mr Clacy at ASU 2 Division, how can I help? Hello…is anyone there…this is ASU 2 Division." The rude sod on the end of the phone had just hung up; clearly they weren't after ASU 2 Division. I then ran back down stairs and found Colin sitting in a small office chair in the kitchen; he was drinking his coffee and said, "I've made you a brew it's on the draining board." No sooner had I picked up my brew when the bloody phone upstairs started ringing again, Colin said, "For fuck's sake mate leave it, let the answer machine get it and phone them back later." I couldn't, it just isn't in my DNA to not answer a phone that is ringing. I said, "No, I'll have to answer it mate." I again ran up the stairs to pick up the phone and got there before the answer machine kicked in on the fourth ring, "Hello ASU 2 Division, Mr Clacy speaking, how can I help?" The rude bastard hung up again and I was starting to get a bit pissed off with whoever it was, they could at least say, "Sorry, I've phoned the wrong number." As I walked back down the stairs I started chuntering, "For fuck's sake Colin, there are some ignorant people in the Civil Service, that's the second time they've just hung up." As I walked into the kitchen the phone upstairs started ringing for the third time, I said to Colin, "For fucks sake mate, they have to be taking the piss"! I turned round to start running up the stairs again and caught the sight of Colin smirking, in his right hand down the side of the chair he was sitting in; he had my telephone number keyed into his mobile telephone. Every time I walked down the stairs he just hit the re-dial button. The twat nearly fell off his chair laughing.

HYPOS

Before my doctor started me on the flexi-pen insulin's that I am using today, I used insulin that was premixed in vials and I needed to eat at set times, I used to have two injections a day, one just before breakfast and the other just before my evening meal. The problem with the old types of insulin was that with a 12-hour regime of insulin a diabetic had to eat at certain times like mid-morning and lunchtime, if you missed these snacks and mealtimes a diabetic's blood sugar would drop quite rapidly and could lead to a hypoglycaemic attack. An ideal mid-morning snack would be an apple or similar piece of fruit; however, during busy days at work a vanilla cream filled doughnut was definitely a more satisfying replacement. In the event of not taking on sufficient carbohydrates and the Blood Glucose dropping below 6.0 mml, then a hypoglycaemic attack will happen and if remained un-treated the diabetic will become very confused and could become unconscious and slip into a coma. If you can get a hypoglycaemic diabetic to eat a chocolate bar whilst they are at the confused stage, you can save yourself and the diabetic a whole lot of grief. I have had quite a few hypos during my time as a diabetic (see 'Harry was a Crap Hat' for further reading on this subject) but one of the worst was during my time as an ASA at Leconfield.

My brilliant line manager 'Tug' Wilson (he was one of only a handful of really good ASU managers) was carrying out his part of an annual Logistical Support Inspection at Leconfield, all units in the MOD have their vehicles, fuel, rations, ammunition and accommodation stores accounts inspected every year to make sure all rules and regulations are rigorously adhered too. 'Tug' was a 5 foot 5 inch dark haired Durham man with a potbelly, he was a North Eastern man through and through and he didn't stand on ceremony, he wouldn't call a mistake a mistake, he would call a mistake "A total fooken cock oop man"! Colonel or Corporal, Brigadier or Bombardier; everyone was treated the same by 'Tug'. Colin, the senior storekeeper at Accommodation Stores in Leconfield once came up to my units' Headquarters in Catterick with me and met 'Tug' for the first time. After introducing Colin to my boss; 'Tug' firmly shook Colin's hand and then sat down in his large managers style swivel chair, he then put his feet up on his desk and shoved his hand down the front of his trousers and started scratching his balls, he nodded towards a kettle on a tray in the corner of the room and said, "Howay Colin man, put the fooken kettle on". 'Tug' briefly left his office to answer a query with another member of staff and Colin leaned over to me and said, "I'm glad he shook my hand before he scratched his balls."

After carrying out his inspection, I took 'Tug' down to the Quartermasters Office which was just a couple of minutes' walk away from Accommodation Stores, Staff Sergeant 'Shuggy' Hughes who was the Accommodation Stores SQMS (Squadron Quartermaster Sergeant), accompanied us so the four of us could discuss any accommodation stores problems and sign up the paperwork. After walking into the Quartermasters office I became very confused when the QM asked me to take a seat, my blood sugar was dropping rapidly because we had done a lot of running around the camp visiting several account areas and I hadn't had anything to eat since breakfast. I picked up a chair and asked the QM, in all sincerity, where he wanted me to take it, the QM politely laughed at what he thought was my pathetic attempt at an old joke. 'Tug' was also a diabetic and he recognised that I was going hypoglycaemic, "He's gannen haypo Cornel, aye think someones should tek him back tay the office reet noow and get him summat tay eat like, are yuz alrayt Harry man?" No I wasn't alright. I was sweating profusely and behaving like a slower than average buffoon when 'Shuggy' ushered me out of the QM's office and tried to guide me back up the road to Accommodation Stores. Half way back I collapsed in the road and 'Shuggy' went into serious panic mode, "For fucks sake Harry, I'm not used to this sort of thing, tell me what you need me to do"! Being semi-conscious and incoherent I was unable to give 'Shuggy' any re-assurance or medical advice on how to deal with my low blood sugar, he might as well have tried asking a blind, deaf and dumb man to explain how the internal combustion engine works. We were joined by a couple of women who took charge and telephoned for an ambulance; Shuggy came up with a plan of action whilst my helpers waited for the paramedics to arrive. "Colin knows how to deal with Harry, he's seen him have loads of these fits, I'll go and get him"! Even today I am still bemused that 'Shuggy' could totally misdiagnosed my diabetes with epilepsy. Still, as he said, he wasn't used to this sort of thing.

He ran up the road and into the Accommodation Stores office where he found Colin hard at work on his computer playing 'Freecell', "Colin! Harry has collapsed outside, we've called for an ambulance but he's going into a coma, what should we do"! Without looking up from his card game Colin said, "Oh for fucks sake not again! That man really is a pain in the arse"! 'Shuggy' started shouting,

"This is not the time to be flippant Colin, your friend is lying passed out on the road and in need of some serious help, now what the fuck do we need to do." Colin turned towards 'Shuggy' and said, "For Christ's sake calm down, just shove a Mars bar down his throat", to which 'Shuggy' asked, "Isn't that dangerous?" In his usual sarcastic way Colin smiled and replied, "Not as long as you keep your fingers clear of his teeth"!

TRACY GETS CAUGHT OUT

Tracy Carter was an ASA who worked down at RAF Kirton Lindsey in Lincolnshire; she was a part of the same ASU unit as me but covered a different area. After yet another Civil Service re-shuffle our new Line Manager was now based on the other side of the country in Lancashire and our main Headquarters had now moved from Catterick Garrison in Yorkshire to Sterling in Scotland. It was now therefore difficult for any of our management dickheads to sneak up and catch us out skiving; if they wanted to visit any particular ASA in their area they would have to arrange a prior appointment to make sure we didn't have any other meetings that involved us being absent from the office. One of our senior ASU management was an ex- RAOC officer and he was actually born in the land of porridge gobblers, an unpleasant snide of a man who took every opportunity to chide any Civil Servants he decreed as inferior to him. We were all spoken to like Private soldiers under his command and I have never heard of anyone praising or passing compliments on this vile and uncouth tyrant.

Any ASA who was out of their office had to leave a message on their answer machine stating where they were at that time and how they could be contacted, because Tracy's Married Quarters' were spread over a large area she was given an ASU mobile telephone which, unfortunately for her, meant she was contactable by the tyrant at all times of the day. Tracy had served in the Civil Service for many years in many countries, Cyprus, Canada and Germany to name but a few, she knew the score on how the MOD worked and how to play the game. Tracy had decided not to apply for any more overseas positions and gave up the Civil Service nomad life, after being selected for the ASA position in Kirton Lindsey she bought a house only a couple of miles from the camp where she worked. The house was quite old and she set about getting it fully refurbished by her dad and his other associated building tradesmen. During the refurbishment a leak had started from some pipes in the loft and Tracy's dad was busy trying to contain the water and stop any further damage, he quickly phoned Tracy who was at work and asked her to nip into B&Q for some urgent parts that he required to stop and repair the leak. Tracy left her office and set off for the B&Q warehouse in Scunthorpe which was about 30 minutes' drive away, she took the ASU mobile phone with her just in case one of her occupants or anyone from the ASU tried to get in contact. As she rushed up and down the aisles in B&Q trying to find the equipment that her dad required, the ASU mobile phone started ringing in her handbag. She took it out and saw from the incoming call display that it was the tyrant phoning her, Tracy quietly cursed, "Oh Bollocks". If caught out of her office the tyrant would want a reasonable excuse for her not being at his beck and call in her place of work, when asked where she was Tracy thought on her feet and told the tyrant, "I'm just in one of my vacant Married Quarters removing all the junk mail that has started to pile up, was it anything urgent you required?" Before the tyrant had a chance to speak, the tannoy in the store loudly rang out, "BING BONG, ELECTRICAL STAFF REQUIRED IN AISLE THREE, ANY SPARE ELECTICAL STAFF PLEASE RESPOND TO A CUSTOMER ENQUIRY IN AISLE THREE PLEASE!"

WHERE'S DAVE GONE?

Colin and I went up to the Distribution Outlet in Catterick Garrison to collect some stores; the DO was like a massive Post Office collection point for all military stores in the 2nd Division area and my ASU unit ran it. We had to collect two small packages of stores for the Quartermasters Department at the Defence School of Transport in Leconfield; Colin was issued with a unit Transit van to do the collection and he asked me if I would like to accompany him on the boring 4 hour round trip. Strictly speaking I shouldn't have gone with him because I wasn't a member of DST; my boss up in Scotland also would have had a dizzy fit if he knew that I was joy riding around North Yorkshire and stopping off at a nice café to have a full English breakfast at lunchtime. I remember thinking at the time, 'Fuck him'! We didn't get to leave Leconfield till 10 o'clock and subsequently arrived at the DO just as the Outlet Staff were heading off to lunch; we approached a small reception office at the side of one of the ramps where all the huge delivery wagons unloaded their cargo. Colin and I wanted to collect the packages before heading off for our full English; we were nothing if not diligent, conscientious, and loyal Civil Servants who were both mindful of carrying out our duties before thinking of ourselves. We also didn't want to be late back to Leconfield because we always finished early on a Friday.

The bloke manning the office was an 18 stone he-man with long greasy hair, tattoos and sleeveless denim jacket, he looked mean and moody (the sort of man whose pint you definitely wouldn't want to spill), he was a dead ringer for an American Hells Angel. Colin and I politely knocked on the door, walked in and said, "Hello, we are from DST Leconfield, we've come to collect some small packages for the QM's Department, can you help us…please"? You should never judge a book by its cover, the man's face broke into a friendly smile and he said in a high pitched Joe Pasquale voice, "Ooh! Hello lads, you need to speak to Dave, you might find him in room 17 just over there". Biting our lips we crossed the gangway and headed for room 17 and knocked on the door before walking in. Room 17 was oblong in shape and had about twenty chairs that were placed around the edge of the room and faced into the centre, on each sacred and reserved chair sat a labourer from the DO with a 'pack-up' balanced on each knee, not one of them was engaged in any sort of conversation. They were all heavily engrossed in devouring their cheese and pickle sandwiches, salt and vinegar crisps and pork pies. As Colin and I entered their rest room the munching stopped and they all looked up quizzically at these 'strangers' who had entered their very private and sacrosanct world. We half expected one of them to say, "Don't go on the moors"! As we were of no interest to them they all carried on stuffing their faces. I looked around each face hoping to find a modicum of intelligence on at least one of them, "Hello, we are from DST Leconfield and have come to pick up a couple of small packages, the guy in the reception told us to speak to Dave". One of the more confident Neanderthals re-looked up and grunted, "He's at lunch" before continuing with his lunch. Not put off by his terse reply we asked if anyone else could help us gain access to DST's packages, his next response was equally brusque, "You need to talk to Dave and he's at lunch." I asked another question purely because I now wanted to stop this ignoramus from eating his food and hopefully annoy him solely by interrupting his gob-stuffing activities. Strangely, even by my standards of sarcasm, my voice suddenly adopted a Lord Snooty accent, "Could you possibly inform me as to when David will be returning from his luncheon?" You probably won't believe this but I swear on my son's life, the ignoramus turned to his left and asked the bloke sitting next to him, "What time are you back from lunch Dave?" Without looking up at Colin and me, Dave briefly stopped filling his cavernous mouth with bad cholesterol and then turned to his mate and said "I won't be back until 1 o'clock", he then carried on eating his food. My original communicator looked up at us and incredulously said, "Dave won't be back from lunch till 1 o'clock". Cue music from 'The Twilight Zone'.

ROYAL MARINES DIVISION

The Defence School of Transport based at Normandy Barracks in Leconfield is a couple of miles north of Beverley in East Yorkshire, the servicemen who train there are all in the driver trade and come from all parts of the British Armed Forces. The bulk of trainees are soldiers from the Royal Logistic Corps doing their basic heavy goods licences, but Airmen from the Royal Air Force and Infantrymen from all regiments, including the Parachute Regiment and SAS, are also trained at Normandy Barracks. Royal Marines are also tutored at Leconfield to prepare them for driving specialised vehicles on exercise in Norway; the Marines are all usually down to earth guys with a good sense of humour. Not long after taking over the job as ASA at Leconfield I went over to the Royal Marines Division; their Company Sergeant Major, WO 2 'Jal' Jenner, had asked me to look at the student desks in his classrooms to see if I could replace them for some larger ones. I liked 'Jal', he was a cheerful Londoner who treated everyone with respect but he could rip out your very soul with his witty sarcasm, I liked him despite the fact he was an avid Chelsea Football Club fan and because he always told me that "West Ham United have always played attractive football." I didn't need to look at the desks though; because 'Jal' was such a nice bloke I would automatically have tried to get him exactly what he needed for his lads. I did go through the motions of examining the Royal Marines desks though because every time I visited 'Jal's' department I was always guaranteed a good cup of tea, a chocolate digestive and a good laugh. Which of the following points do you think helped 'Jal' get exactly what he wanted? Do you think it was because?
He was a really decent bloke.

He always gave me a chocolate digestive with my cup of tea.
He always complimented West Ham United Football Club.
Or was it a combination of all of the above.

If you think it was the last statement to my questionnaire then you are clearly a very perceptive person, well done.

Several years later it was a totally different story. Colin and I went across to see the new CSM of the Marines Division after a garbled phone message was left on Colin's answer machine; the message mentioned something about a new desk being required. We went upstairs and about half way along the corridor on the left hand side was the CSM's office, I knocked on the open door and saw an athletic looking soldier with his back to us crouched over the open bottom draw of a filing cabinet. After we knocked on the door the crouched soldier roared at 300 decibels, 'WAIT', then without turning round to see who we were; he continued on with his search in the bottom drawer. He eventually got up and turned towards Colin and me; on realising we were civilians he put on his best sneer and said, "What do you two want?" My initial thought was, 'you arrogant son of a bitch', I knew Colin was thinking much worse. "I don't want anything from you" I told him, "but I believe your unit needs something from me, we've had a call about some-one needing a desk." The CSM then commanded, "Oh yes, what I want is a new workstation, this desk is hardly fitting for a man in my position and the desk with my computer on over there (he pointed to another desk in the corner of the room) isn't even an IT desk so you'll have to exchange that as well. I want this done by tomorrow!" I pointed out the fact that the desk he was working from was an IT desk and yet it didn't have a computer on it, so why didn't he just put his computer on his main desk and return the other desk to Accommodation Stores. I also pointed out that if he organised his office a bit better he could cover all the bases. This seemed to upset him a little bit and he turned the colour of a London bus as his blood pressure went through the roof in a very short space of time. Through gritted teeth he explained, "I don't want a computer on my desk when people stand to attention in front of me and I want a desk more befitting a Company Sergeant Major in the Royal Marines!" I replied in my Frankie Howard voice, "Oooh dear".

It was at this point that his telephone rang and my fun was temporarily interrupted, the caller was a friend of the CSM and he indulged in a conversation for the next five minutes about where they and their wives were going to eat that night before going to the cinema at Kingswood near Hull. Colin and I stood in the doorway to his office for the duration of his call; the call was so long that the CSM sat down at his desk so he could continue his tête-à-tête more comfortably. Colin nudged me and nodded towards the exit, I shook my head and whispered, "No mate, let's be professional." After hanging up the phone the CSM turned to us and said, "Where was I? Oh yes, that's what I need so get back to me when you need access to my office to deliver the new desk." I disappointed him I'm afraid, "You won't be getting a new desk because this one is a perfectly serviceable IT desk, you just need to reorganise your office a bit better." The CSM then bought the big guns to bear as he waved us out of his office, "Forget about it, you can leave now, I will go above your head and speak to the Quartermaster and arrange my requirements through him."

Colin blurted out in restrained anger, "You can speak to the bloody Commandant as well if you like, the only man on this camp who can authorise and obtain a new desk for you is my colleague Mr Clacy here, and in fact Mr Clacy tells the Quartermaster and Commandant what they can and cannot have." We then left the Royal Marines Division and went back to my office.

At what point do you the reader think I had decided this obnoxious arse wasn't going to get his much desired new Gucci desk? Was it:
When he roared "WAIT!"
When he had his 5 minute tête-à-tête on the telephone.
When he said, "What do you two want?"
or was it when he told me he would speak to the Quartermaster.

If you guessed the first answer to my questionnaire then you are the sort of shrewd and perceptive person of whom I would definitely have given a new desk. I probably don't need to tell you, but I will for the sake of clarification, it wasn't until the day prior to this prick being posted away from Leconfield that I phoned him up and said, "Can you inform your replacement that I will be exchanging his desk for a new one, I will come over to his office with my catalogues so he can make his choice. Thank you".

ONE LAST NUISANCE PHONE CALL

I had an inkling my time in the Civil Service would soon be coming to an end, the MOD (Ministry of Defence) were making noises about getting rid of some of their civilian staff who were felt to be surplus to requirements. It was widely believed that some of the first MOD cuts would be made within the Accommodation Services Units, over the years we had pissed off plenty of people in the Civil Service and it was now pay back time by those higher up the chain of command. The popular census of opinion was that all ASU's were now going to be severely curtailed and our job spec would be shared between the Quartermasters Department and the Defence Housing Establishment. At this time there was also a moratorium on all spending on furniture by every ASU, for about twelve months we couldn't buy any new furniture and this made us even more unpopular with Quartermaster Departments and the occupants of our Married Quarters.

The lads at our distribution warehouse at Catterick ASU had to use and recycle a lot of old stock for our Married Quarters, these furnishings were often angrily rejected by the Service Personnel moving into our houses but there was nothing we could do about it, we as a department hadn't got any money to replace even stained mattresses. I ended up using some of the brand new stock of unit mattresses that were only supposed to be supplied to DST Leconfield, the mattresses were waterproof, foam filled and of a poorer quality than the usual interior sprung type, they were supposed to be used by single soldiers living in barracks but at least they were clean. When given the option of their children sleeping on one of these, or an old and stained

Interior Sprung mattress, most occupants took a realistic stance and were very grateful for my help. However, some of the others created an almighty fuss and the fact that I was breaking all the rules to help them counted for nothing. You can't please everyone.

It wasn't all doom and gloom though because Colin and I had a lot of fun at our new SQMS's expense, SSgt Eddie ward RLC was a man of diminutive stature but he was big in heart, he was also affected with a bad case of the tight fistedness. He kept such a tight grip on his 'my little pony' purse that not even Hercules himself could have got him to buy an egg and bacon butty from the NAAFI. Eddie made the mistake of telling us that he once failed to complete his Royal Marine training and selection course; after a short period of time back in Civvy Street he re-enlisted back into the forces, but this time in the Royal Corps of Transport. Every time one of the Commando's from the Royal Marines Division in Leconfield came over to accommodation stores, Colin would always introduce Eddie thus, "Have you met our new SQMS SSgt Eddie Ward, he once trained to be a Royal Marine like you…but unlike you he failed miserably because…boo hoo, it was just too hard". Eddie took it all in good stead though and eventually learned to keep his mouth shut in front of Colin, especially when talking about something he didn't want to be of general piss taking knowledge. It was shortly before Eddie was due to leave the army that he became accustomed to me and Colin and our mickey taking ways, we always referred to him as the 'Royal Marine Reject' or our 'Green Machine Dwarf'.

Eddie asked me one day if I could do a prank call to a friend of his, this friend used to be Eddie's old Troop Commander when he was serving with 8 Regiment RLC out in Germany. Always willing to oblige I agreed and Eddie filled me in on the background information that I needed to make the hoax call. His old Troop Commander is now a Major and Squadron Commander in the Royal Logistic Corps so I have therefore used a pseudonym to save his dignity and career as an officer and gentleman in the British Army. Captain Ray Fullerton was 2i/c of an RLC Squadron whilst serving out in Afghanistan and at the time of this background information he was based in Camp Bastion, Ray was and is an extremely fit young officer who often trained with Eddie over in the lake district, they were so fit that the pair of them used to run up and down Scafell Pike, but Captain Ray Fullerton always led the way and set an extremely fast pace. From Ray and Eddie's hotel at the Holbeck Ghyll Country House Hotel it would take an average, but fit person, 3 to 3 1/2 hours to get to the top of Scafell Pike. Ray and Eddie usually did the climb in two hours.

Whilst out in Afghanistan this handsome and extremely fit young officer started to have a romantic liaison with a female Full Corporal from his Squadron, Corporal Helen Buckle RLC was known to be attracted to the more macho type of soldiers like Paratroopers and Royal Marines. It was Ray's turn to satisfy this energetic young woman's needs and although an Officer and Junior NCO relationship would automatically get him the sack, they both banged each other's brains out during the tour. Ray was due to leave the Squadron on a new posting after the tour in Afghanistan was completed, but he wouldn't be taking up his new post before going on leave to the United States for a couple of weeks. Two weeks in America with his outstandingly beautiful blonde haired girlfriend was exactly what Ray needed after the fraught and tough tour he had just been through. His fortnight holiday location turned out to be a bit of a war zone in itself though, Ray rather stupidly gave Corporal Helen Buckle RLC his email address before departing Afghanistan so they could keep in touch, he also lent his lap top computer to his outstandingly beautiful blonde haired girlfriend for a couple of days on their break out in the States. Guess who sent him a more than suggestive email message that his outstandingly beautiful blonde haired girlfriend opened. Officers? I fucking ask you. (Authors note: Don't worry readers, Ray has recovered from his traumatic break-up and I have met his NEW outstandingly beautiful blonde haired girlfriend.

Meanwhile back at the ranch, Eddie mentioned these facts to me and wondered if I could come up with a good wind up for his friend and Ex Troop Commander. Eddie, Colin, WO 2 Dave Hall (DST's RQMS), and several other DST soldiers gathered round to listen to me as I phoned the Abingdon Military Telephone number that Eddie had given me, I heard Ray's brusque officer telephone manner as he answered the call at the other end. The following conversation continued with me adopting a Noel Coward type accent:

Ray: "Major Fullerton!"

Me: "Oh Good morning Major Fullerton, this is Captain Smyth, Army Welfare up in Catterick Garrison, how are you today."

Ray: "Fine, what can I do for you Captain Smyth?"

Me: "You are going to have to forgive me because this is a rather delicate telephone call, I've been handed this hot potato and I don't wish to cause you any embarrassment or humiliation but this is a distasteful chore that has been well and truly dumped in my lap. I hope you will bear with me. I believe your name is Ray, would you mind awfully if I called you Ray, I think it would be so much nicer to talk on an informal basis, don't you? My name is Reginald."

Ray: "Certainly, but this all sounds a bit ominous Reginald, what is the problem?"

Me: "I believe you returned from an operational tour in Afghanistan about eight months ago, can you confirm that for me?"

Ray: "Yes that's right."

Me: "Thank you for that, can you also confirm that during the tour you were serving as 2i/c of an RLC Squadron in Camp Bastion?"

Ray: "Er, yes I was, I can't see exactly where this conversation is heading, why do you want to know about my tour in Afghanistan?"

Me: "I'm so sorry but if you could just bear with me for a couple of more questions and I'm sure everything will become crystal clear."

Ray: Yes, I'm so sorry, do go on."

Me: Was Corporal Helen Buckle of the Royal Logistic Corps one of the soldiers serving under you during your tour in Camp Bastion?"

Ray: (Silence)

Me: Hello! Major Fullerton? Are you there?

Ray: Oh yes, I'm still here, ahm...yes Corporal Buckle was one of my Section Commanders in the Squadron, has something happened to her?"

Me: No no, she's fine and dandy; in fact she is one of the soldiers under my care up here in Catterick Garrison."

Ray: "Oh good, please do pass on my kindest regards to her would you?"

Me: "Erm...yes of course, I'll tell her you were asking after her... it's actually Sergeant Buckle now, and it is her that I needed to talk to you about...she's about to give birth in the next few weeks."

Ray: (Silence)

Me: Hello! Ray? Are you there?

Ray: (Silence)

Me: Hello... I think there's a fault on this line...Major Fullerton can you hear me?"

Ray: "Yes! Yes! I can hear you. Erm, I didn't know that Sergeant Buckle had got married after getting back from Afghanistan?"

Me: "Well that is the unfortunate thing Ray old boy, she isn't married and I'm sure you are now aware of where our conversation is heading."

Ray: (I swear I actually heard a gulp on the end of the line).

Me: I'm so sorry to have to ask you this Major..sorry I mean Ray, but did you have a relationship with Sergeant Buckle whilst you were both serving out in Afghanistan?"

Ray: "Erm…well…we actually became very good friends out in Afghanistan and became quite close…yes I suppose we did have a close relationship…erm…whilst we...erm… were in Camp Bastion."

Me: "But did you have, and I'm really sorry to be so blunt old boy, sexual relations with Sergeant Buckle."

Ray: (I could hear the cogs in Ray's head whirring and grinding away like those in a chainsaw mill)

Me: "Please don't worry Ray old boy, you are only one of four in the frame for this, we are hoping you will agree to having a DNA test to eliminate you from our enquires, I mean there is a 75% chance that you are not the father of Helen's baby, let's all keep our fingers crossed eh."

Eddie, Colin and WO 2 Dave Hall all stopped sniggering and burst out laughing, Eddie took the phone off me and said, "For fuck's sake Harry, you'll have to stop before Ray shit's his pants." Ray recognised Eddie's voice and all I heard from the telephone receiver was, "Ward, you fucking bastard." To this day Eddie and Ray remain very good friends, but from Ray's perspective, I do wonder why.

EPILOGUE

Well, it did happen in the end, apart from a handful of ASA's around the UK all the others were picked out for VERS (Voluntary Early Release Scheme), which was a posh way of telling us we were being made redundant. I'm not complaining about it though because personally it was a perfect opportunity for me to enter early retirement at 55 years of age, Nicky and I cashed in our Endowment policies a couple of years earlier than planned and used a small a portion of my redundancy…sorry, I mean VERS money, to pay off our mortgage. We also had a full army and a war pension paid into our bank account every month, so life was sweet in the Clacy household. I took six months off and stuck my thumb up my bum and put my mind into neutral. Nicky was still working at the Tourist Information Centre in Beverley at the time and after I waved her off to work I went back to bed for a couple of hours, I didn't think 11 o'clock in the morning was an unreasonable time to get up out of bed and face the world. Having said that I began to worry when I started watching the Jeremy Kyle show in my pyjamas, I was becoming a mentally redundant piece of human effluence.

I am by nature a social animal and I have to have human contact, every day humanoid conversation is the very bread and butter of my existence. I had to get a job or the men in white coats would soon be coming to take me away and lock me up for my own safety. It is a common enough phrase that you hear, "Oh I would love to retire early but I just can't afford it." Trust me people, if you do retire at the age of 55 years old, you will more than likely find that it's a poisoned chalice. Jeremy Kyle and his bated council estate dancing bears will not fill your life with contentment; make sure before retiring that you at least have some interests, hobbies or goals in your life. If you don't, you'll go nuts.

My life has been full of laughter with the odd bit of misery thrown in to balance things out, my mum and dad both had unsurpassed senses of humour, as did my siblings. Trisha has lived near St Andrews Golf Club up in Bonnie Scotland for the past few decades; Susan lives over in Winsford in Cheshire and is now a qualified State Registered nurse, and my brother David still lives down in Chelmsford in Essex. He used to be a presenter on Radio Essex but gave all that up to earn a more lucrative wage as a Gas and Plumbing Engineer. My dad died whilst I was still serving in the army and stationed at Bordon in Hampshire in the late 1980's, dad was suffering from atheroma which meant all his arteries were blocked and his heart was trying to pump blood with the consistency of treacle around his body. He had worked hard all his life and eventually died at the age of 65, just a matter of weeks after retiring from the Prison Service. The Ambulance Technicians who dealt with my dad's heart attack stated that he was probably dead even before he fell face down on the beach whilst walking his new wife's dog. I never told you this dad, but as a young child I used to think of you as a British version of John Wayne, I was always proud of the fact that you were a soldier, and a far better one than I could ever have been.

Mum divorced dad while we were living in Chelmsford after he had run away with another prison officer's wife and he got a posting to Wormwood Scrubs Prison in London. Poor old mum was devastated but she eventually remarried a Yorkshire man and moved up to Leeds with him. I had lost contact with my mum for various reasons, none of which she was ever at fault, but I contacted her as I was in the process of divorcing my ex-wife, mum was by this stage living in Bradford. She bizarrely asked me if I would mind if she and her new husband moved over and lived in Beverley to be near me, the council provided them with a lovely little flat where Nicky and I often visited her. Within a couple of years my mum started to look thinner and drawn in her face and so she went to see her doctor. She was admitted to the Princess Royal Cancer Hospital in Hull, she had cancer of the stomach. After having an exploratory operation the surgeon in the hospital told my mum she had secondary cancers. Trisha and I were with her when she was told, my mum calmly asked the doc, "So is that it then, are you telling me my cancer is terminal." The doctor confirmed that it was and unfortunately my poor old mum never got to leave that hospital again before she died, Trisha, Susan, David and I were at mum's bedside when she passed away. She never once complained about her terminal illness and always smiled every time she was visited, my God I hope I can be that brave and have that amount of dignity when my time comes. I knew my mum was tough, any unescorted married woman who had to sail half way around the world from Hong Kong back to England on a troop ship, whilst caring for two young children in the late 1950's, definitely had to be resilient. But mum's bravery and fortitude whilst dealing with this awful malignancy absolutely astounded me. That was in 2005 and there are so many questions I would have liked to have asked my mum and dad, but it is too late now. I'm so sorry mum; I could have been a much better son.

About a year before I was made redundant I was speaking to my neighbour Ken Baines as he restored his MGBGT outside the front of his house. Ken has his own business in Hull called East Riding Training Solutions, he trains and tests Gas, Electrical, Plumbing and Solar Power engineers. ERTS is a family run business with Ken as the CEO and owner, his daughter Jill is the Finance Director and Chris his son is an assessor, IT wizard, and along with his dad, a font of all knowledge on anything to do with the above subjects. I told Ken, "I think the MOD is going to make me redundant and I'm a little unsure of what I'm going to do with the rest of my life." 'Harry was a Crap Hat' was starting to sell quite well but 'Two Medics One Nurse and a Gob Doctor' still wasn't ready for publication, the book was originally going to be called 'Three Medics One Nurse and a Gob Doctor', but one of the medics pulled out at the last minute because he was still serving in the RAMC. He was under a threat from the MOD of being cashiered out of the Officers Mess if his stories were published. I love writing but didn't know if I could make a living out of it, I'm not the most disciplined of writers and I can be easily distracted.

Ken offered me a part-time job as an invigilator at his training centre and so with a certain amount of trepidation, I started overseeing his Gas Engineer candidates and checking their answer sheet grids when they were going through the non-practical tests. With the plethora of British Standard Publications that are used during this testing period, there was a lot to learn but the majority of the Hull based men that come in for testing, are a collective encyclopaedia of Northern hilarity. I now look forward to going to work every Monday and Tuesday just to see who will be the next comedian sitting his gas re-assessment exams. In return for giving me a job, Nicky and I agreed to go on holiday with the Baines family and I gave them a conducted First World

War tour round the battlefields of Ypres in Belgium and the Somme in France. I try to visit Belgium and France at least once a year and I generally go with some mates of mine, if I took Nicky there for ten days she would definitely end up sticking a bayonet in my neck. As a result of my many previous visits there, I have an intricate knowledge of the First and Second World Wars and their Geography in Europe; I have subsequently learned where the best places are to visit.

In August of 2013 the Clacy and Baines families are off to Normandy to 'do a bit of the Second World War' under my guidance, it is one of the few situations in life where, 'Harry Isn't Always a Crap Hat'.

Printed in Great Britain
by Amazon